REACH

REACH

How to Build Confidence and

Step Outside Your Comfort Zone

ANDY MOLINSKY, PHD

PENGUIN LIFE

AN IMPRINT OF

PENGUIN BOOKS

PENGUIN LIFE

UK | USA | Canada | Ireland | Australia
India | New Zealand | South Africa

Penguin Life is part of the Penguin Random House group of companies
whose addresses can be found at global.penguinrandomhouse.com.

First published in the United States of America by Avery, an imprint
of Penguin Random House LLC 2017
First published in Great Britain by Penguin Life 2017
001

Printed in Great Britain by Clays Ltd, St Ives plc

A CIP catalogue record for this book is available from the British Library

ISBN: 978-0-241-25132-4

www.greenpenguin.co.uk

Penguin Random House is committed to a
sustainable future for our business, our readers
and our planet. This book is made from Forest
Stewardship Council® certified paper.

For Alice, Ben, and Jen—
who inspire me in my own efforts to step
outside my comfort zone.

Contents

Introduction   1

PART I

The Challenge of Reaching Outside
Your Comfort Zone

CHAPTER 1   Why Reaching Outside Your
Comfort Zone Is So Hard   23

CHAPTER 2   Our Amazing Capacity to Avoid   55

PART II

How to Successfully Reach Outside
Your Comfort Zone

CHAPTER 3   Conviction: The Critical Importance
of Having a Deep Sense of Purpose   75

CHAPTER 4 Customization: Finding Your Own
Personal Way of Performing the Task   89

CHAPTER 5 Clarity: The Power of Honest
Perspective   127

CHAPTER 6 The Surprising Benefits of
Taking a Leap   145

PART III

How to Make Your New Behavior Stick

CHAPTER 7 Building Resilience   177

CHAPTER 8 The Myths and Realities   213

PART IV

Practical Tools: Applying *Reach* to Your Own Life

Notes   255

Acknowledgments   267

Index   271

Introduction

Lily Chang paced back and forth around her office. She took a bite of a muffin but put it down. She didn't feel hungry at all, even though she hadn't eaten all day. She nervously checked her phone. No messages. She then checked her pulse. Sky-high—around 95 or 98 beats a minute. It was a year since Lily had started her Internet company and six months after she had hired her best friend, Julia. And now Lily had to do the unthinkable and actually tell her friend that she no longer had a job. And as Lily continued pacing around the room, thinking of things to say and then immediately rejecting all of them, she thought to herself that she honestly had no idea if she could actually go through with it.

No one likes to move beyond their comfort zone, but

as the saying goes, that's where the magic happens. It's where we can grow, learn, and develop in a way that expands our horizons beyond what we thought was possible. Also, it's terrifying. In Lily's case, she had to fire her best friend. But all of us confront tasks at work that force us outside our comfort zones. It may not be firing a best friend, but it could be giving negative feedback, or promoting ourselves, or speaking up, or networking. The list of uncomfortable but necessary tasks is long—and unfortunately quite challenging. And although these small things seem irksome, no one ever succeeds at a high level or accomplishes substantial goals without learning to confront them.

Take, for example, the case of Neil Kennedy, who, before Facebook even existed, had a Facebook-like website that could have potentially revolutionized the Internet. But Neil was shy and inexperienced, and the idea of walking into a room to pitch his product—and himself— to a group of high-octane investors was overwhelming. In the end, Neil went into avoidance mode, tweaking and perfecting his website for such a long time that Facebook itself eventually launched and his fledgling ideas had become obsolete. He was so afraid of acting outside his comfort zone that he never capitalized on a potentially life-changing opportunity.

A different but equally challenging case comes from Annie Jones, a thirty-four-year-old account manager at a financial firm whose challenge was finding a way to be assertive and direct with a male portfolio manager who would undermine her in client meetings—when her natural tendency was to smooth things over and avoid conflict. Annie tried to "hint" at her frustration, or make a snide remark here or there under her breath. But it didn't go anywhere, and the manager's bad behavior just continued.

In an ideal world, no one would have to reach beyond their comfort zone to succeed at work, and all the tasks and responsibilities we need to perform would fit perfectly with our personalities. Annie would have the confidence and assertiveness to easily confront her colleagues; Neil would have the bravado to present his ideas; and Lily would have the courage, confidence, and resolve to deliver her message.

But unfortunately, this is not usually the case. Conflict-avoidant managers often need to embrace conflict—or at least learn to tolerate it. Timid entrepreneurs need to be able to pitch and promote themselves and their ideas . . . introverts need to network . . . self-conscious executives need to deliver speeches . . . and people pleasers need to deliver bad news. You get the idea.

As we grow and learn and advance in our jobs and in our careers, we're constantly faced with situations where we need to adapt and adjust our behavior. It's simply a reality of the world we work in today. And without the skill—and courage—to take the leap, we can miss out on important opportunities for advancement. Also, like Lily, we can fail to perform the tasks that are critical for advancing our businesses and our careers. And that's where this book comes in. The goal of this book is to give you the tips and tools—not to mention the courage—to take that leap, reach outside your comfort zone, and do it in a way that is both effective and authentic, meeting the expectations you need to achieve and without losing yourself in the process.

Chances are, if you've ever been interested in the topic of comfort zones—and are comfortable with the

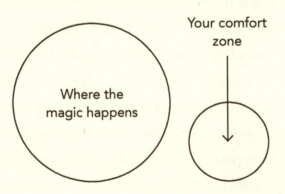

search function on Google—you've come across something like what you see above.

And if you delve further into the world of comfort zones on Google (as I have!), you'll find many other pictures and diagrams of similar ilk. You have brazen goldfish taking the leap and jumping from one fishbowl to another. You have people walking on tightropes, parachuting, jumping off cliffs—telling you that "everything you've always wanted is one step beyond your comfort zone" and that "you're only confined by the walls you build for yourself." And then, of course, there are the stories—successful and confident people who had the courage to go for it, and take a leap, and are now spokespeople for Comfort Zone, Inc., imploring us to do the same: Take the leap! Go for it! The only thing to fear is fear itself!

As you can probably tell, I have always been both inspired by these sorts of messages and frustrated by them. I love the idea that we all have a comfort zone—a place where we feel capable and at ease—but that stretching outside this comfort zone is critical in many cases for achieving our goals—or, in terms of the picture above—to get where the magic happens. That's the fascinating part.

The frustrating part is that I've always felt a bit

hopeless trying to apply this logic to lessons in my own life. And I suspect that others probably have been too. For starters, I've always found the diagram with the two circles representing "your comfort zone" and "where the magic happens" to be extraordinarily incomplete. Where, for example, is the bridge between the two circles? In other words, how do you actually get from one place to another? It's nice to think that it's as easy as a fish jumping from one bowl to another, but I know from personal experience that this simply is not the case. Stretching outside your comfort zone takes serious effort and work. You need motivation for sure—and I do find many of the messages on the Internet to be quite inspirational. But motivation alone doesn't seal the deal. What's truly lacking is a concrete road map about the "how"—how to move from a place of fear, paralysis, and avoidance to the point of actually being willing and able to take that leap and start a more positive cycle of learning and development.

We often feel overwhelmed—sometimes even hopeless—when we have to act outside our comfort zones. But the reality is that we face a set of very predictable and identifiable challenges—and we can overcome these challenges by following the guidelines outlined in this book. This book will explain why it's so hard to act outside your comfort zone and help you develop the courage and ability to flex your behavior with success. The framework in the book is not one size fits all; rather, it is personalized and customized to the particular challenges that you happen to face in any situation you find yourself.

My Own Journey

Probably like many of you, I have been struggling with this issue of behavior flexing throughout my own adult life, sometimes taking a leap and going for it, and other times crafting my life or my job to unfortunately avoid opportunities that could have potentially led to real growth and development. For example, in college, I was afraid of saying anything in class, and therefore ended up choosing mostly lecture-style courses where classroom participation wasn't an important part of the agenda. I was also afraid of stretching my skills and trying something "more professional" outside of school and during the summers, even though I was certainly curious about the "real" world. As a result, I taught tennis and was a summer camp counselor—both were rewarding experiences, but neither really enabled me to explore the world of business, which interested me and, at the same time, felt unfamiliar and scary. In my first job as a professor, I was quite tentative in faculty meetings—just like in college. I wasn't sure what to say, or whether what I thought I wanted to say had any merit. I was also pretty intimidated by the senior faculty, worried they would scrutinize my every word.

And even now, as a senior faculty member at a different school, I feel the struggle of adjusting my behavior in different domains. Public speaking—especially to business audiences—has been a challenge I've had to overcome. It's especially challenging when I have to convince busy executives of the importance of topics like acting outside your comfort zone. I have had to learn to be more direct and authoritative, to project confidence in a way that isn't necessarily my go-to demeanor. I've also had to learn to schmooze and network, when I'd much prefer to meet people one on one over coffee, or even connect via Skype.

I feel like I'm constantly navigating my own personal comfort zone—and from what I hear from others, I know I'm not alone. In fact, as a university professor, I have been studying this topic in one way or another for the past fifteen years. I started this work with a project about organizational change at two distinct types of organizations: a Fortune 500 corporation and a metropolitan teaching hospital. While doing this work, I was struck by the difficulties employees in these organizations experienced during the change process and by how much of that struggle was rooted in having to deviate from intuitive patterns of behavior. In the ensuing years, I became fascinated by this idea of acting outside your comfort zone and studied it in two very different settings.

The first was in the context of having to perform what my research collaborator and I called "necessary evils" at work—situations where people had to cause physical and/or emotional pain and discomfort to others as part of their professional position. We studied managers firing and laying off employees, police officers serving warrants or evicting people from their homes, doctors delivering negative diagnoses to patients or performing painful procedures, and tough-love therapists at addiction facilities humiliating and embarrassing addicts with the goal of rehabilitating them. In each case, the professionals in these settings struggled to perform tasks at work that were necessary in order to achieve the mission of their organization or the responsibilities of their jobs, but that were deeply uncomfortable. And to succeed, they needed to find a way to successfully flex their behavior, ideally in a way that helped them achieve their professional objective but that didn't make them feel like they were losing themselves in the process.

Alongside this work in necessary evils, I have also been deeply involved in studying the process of acting outside your comfort zone in another way: that of adapting and adjusting behavior across cultures. I began this work in the late 1990s with my PhD dissertation, which focused on the difficulties professionals from the former Soviet Union faced when learning how to interview for jobs in the United States. From this project, I coined the term "cross-cultural code-switching," and since that time I have examined the phenomenon of stepping outside your *cultural* comfort zone in a vast array of professional settings. I have interviewed more than seventy-five executives and managers about their experiences switching cultural behavior in a range of different cultures. I have developed training and teaching materials to help people understand and manage the challenges they face when switching cultural behavior. I also recently completed a major research study of professionals from a range of countries and cultures adapting their behavior in the United States. As part of this project, I followed fifty foreign-born professionals as they learned to adapt their behavior over a two-month period. From a careful analysis of the experiences of individuals who thrived compared to those who struggled, I extracted lessons about the core challenges of cross-cultural code-switching and how people can successfully manage these challenges. This work culminated in my first book, *Global Dexterity*, which focused on the challenges of acting outside your cultural comfort zone in various situations.

Ever since the publication of *Global Dexterity*, I have received multiple comments from readers about how the tools and insights in the book apply much more widely than simply to national cultural adaptation. In other words, without realizing it, I had created tools applicable to adaptation in general. Encouraged by this feedback, I wrote a trial balloon Web article for the *Harvard Business Review* titled "Get Out of Your Comfort Zone: A Guide for the Terrified," which turned out to be the most popular post I have done in the past few years. I have also created an MBA course at Brandeis University that focuses on learning how to reach outside your comfort zone—both across cultures and also within one's own culture. As part of the capstone assignment for the course, students choose real situations with which to work on flexing their behavior, and this enables me to view firsthand the challenges they face, as well as how the tools I have created can help them address these challenges. So as you can see, reaching outside your comfort zone—and all the challenges it entails—is something that I've been passionate about for years. And from what I've learned from talking to others, I don't think I'm alone.

What You Will Learn in This Book

Reaching beyond your comfort zone is hard to do, but it's hard for a set of very predictable reasons. Once you recognize these reasons, you can start to develop a plan for addressing them. With that in mind, let me give you a sense of the journey you're about to go on. In Part I of the book, we'll focus on the *challenges* of stretching outside your comfort zone. In fact, we're going to focus on five specific and very common challenges people across professions face when trying to stretch outside their comfort zones.

The first challenge is what I call the authenticity challenge, which occurs when acting outside your comfort zone feels fake, foreign, and false. Neil Kennedy, for example, felt like a fish out of water when he eventually pitched and promoted his ideas to venture capitalists. He put on a suit for the occasion—although he never, ever wore a suit in real life, and as he started talking in his "grown-up" voice, he felt completely inauthentic and un-natural. And it definitely showed.

The second challenge—the likeability challenge—occurs when, as a result of the behavioral stretch you have to make, you fear others won't like you. Annie Jones, for example, worried that if she confronted her colleague, he wouldn't like her anymore. Although in her interview with me Annie herself recognized how illogical that was, it still felt like a significant psychological burden as she contemplated adapting her behavior.

The third challenge—the competence challenge—occurs when you feel you don't actually have the skills or knowledge to perform the new task successfully. As a novice leader, Lily experienced the competence challenge when firing her friend. So did Neil when trying to pitch his ideas to investors. They both felt anxious about their lack of knowledge and skill, and self-conscious that these deficiencies were obvious to others.

The fourth challenge—the resentment challenge—happens when you feel frustrated and annoyed that you have to adapt behavior in the first place. Annie, for example, felt resentful that in addition to the "regular" challenges of her job, she had to expend such consider-able energy and effort confronting the jerk who was ruining her life at work.

Finally, the fifth challenge is the morality challenge: the feeling—logical or illogical—that when stretching your behavior, you will feel inappropriate or perhaps even unethical. Lily felt this challenge acutely when she had to fire her friend. Although she actually believed the firing was necessary and that she was doing everything possible to be as compassionate as she could, deep down she still had doubts that she was doing the right thing.

As you can imagine, any one of these challenges can be burdensome when attempting to reach outside your comfort zone. But when you experience more than one challenge, which is often the case, it can be paralyzing. As a result, many people avoid acting outside their comfort zones altogether, crafting their jobs and their lives to avoid these essential tasks that are just too stressful to consider.

After learning about the challenges, our focus will then turn to developing solutions. We often feel powerless facing situations that we know are critical to our success but are so difficult to perform because they are outside our comfort zones. The reality is that we do have power to overcome these challenges—and this power comes in the form of three essential resources that I introduce in Part II of the book. The first resource is *conviction*. Once you've identified the importance of acting outside your comfort zone and how hard it might be to achieve, you need to develop a deep sense of purpose that it's actually worth it for you to put in the time and effort necessary to make these changes. Without unlocking your own personal source of conviction it's unlikely you will be truly motivated to make behavior change work.

The second resource is *customization*, which is the ability to adjust and tweak the way you perform the task itself to make it more comfortable and natural for you. It's like adapting a recipe to fit your needs, or altering a pair of pants to fit your waist. We often make these slight but meaningful adjustments to personalize things in our lives, and there's no difference with behavior flexing. You can customize the way you perform the behavior itself so it fits just right—or, at least, feels comfortable enough to give it a go.

The third critical resource is *clarity*. One of the greatest challenges to acting outside your comfort zone is exaggerated and negative distorted thinking, where we conjure up all the reasons why we can "never" do the task we're thinking of doing. We focus on our limitations and liabilities . . . when in reality, like many things in life, even challenging situations like this have shades of gray. We might genuinely struggle with certain elements of a situation, but, perhaps, actually find other parts exciting or interesting or possible. Clarity is the ability to take an honest psychological accounting of our likes and dislikes about a particular situation, our strengths and weaknesses, and to do so without letting distorted thinking hijack our "rational selves."

Of course it's great to get over the hump in a particular situation and muster up the courage to act outside your comfort zone. But it's even better to keep up the momentum and translate initial attempts into a more enduring skill. In the final section of the book, Part IV, we'll examine the practices you can put into place in order to make your behavior change stick.

In the process of doing research for this book, I've interviewed people across many professions and have also combed research and popular literature to gain additional insights and examples to enrich the discussion. In these pages, you'll hear from managers, executives, and entrepreneurs, and from rabbis, priests, and doctors. You'll hear from students and professors grappling with their comfort zones in academic settings, baristas struggling to make small talk, and stay-at-home moms struggling to learn how to network and promote themselves when taking the leap back into the marketplace. You'll hear from actors and composers, singers and writers, comics and politicians—some famous, some not—all working in some way to step outside their comfort zones. The stories are different, but the themes are the same.

No one ever said getting outside your comfort zone is easy. It takes time, effort, strategy, and determination. My sincere wish is that, with the tools and techniques you will read about in this book, along with inspirational stories from people just like you who have confronted and ultimately overcome their behavior flexing challenges, you will have the courage and confidence to change behavior in your own life. I hope you'll come along for the ride!

PART I

The Challenge
of Reaching Outside
Your Comfort Zone

It's fairly obvious that acting outside your comfort zone is challenging and that it takes a leap of faith and courage to do. But what might not be so obvious is exactly *why* it's so challenging. In other words, what is it about acting outside your comfort zone that is so self-threatening, and what, then, can you do to overcome these challenges? So in the first chapter of the book, we'll focus on these core psychological challenges—the reasons why it can be so scary to step outside our comfort zones. Then, in the second chapter, we'll focus on a very common consequence of these challenges: avoidance. As it turns out, we're actually quite creative at finding ways to avoid doing these tasks that are uncomfortable, but also quite critical to our personal and professional well-being.

CHAPTER 1

Why Reaching Outside Your Comfort Zone Is So Hard

Acting outside your comfort zone is difficult to do, but it's difficult for a set of very predictable reasons. Once you understand these reasons, you'll be better equipped to manage them. As I indicated earlier, I've uncovered a set of five core psychological barriers people often face while trying to act outside their comfort zones.

1. The authenticity challenge: the feeling that "This isn't me at all" and the distress that results from that feeling.

2. The likeability challenge: the sense that doing this will "make people not like me," and the worry that results from that perception.

3. The competence challenge: the feeling that "I'm not good at this behavior, and it's obvious to others," along with corresponding feelings of embarrassment and, perhaps, shame.

4. The resentment challenge: the strong sense that I "shouldn't have to be doing this behavior" in the first place, and the frustration and anger that result from that feeling.

5. The morality challenge: the feeling that the behavior isn't something I "should be doing," and the anxiety and guilt that can result from that sense.

You won't necessarily experience all five of these challenges every time you consider acting outside your comfort zone. But, really, any one of these challenges can be enough to make this very hard to do. Ahead, we'll talk about the creative ways we find to avoid acting outside our comfort zones (in part, to avoid these feelings), but for now, let's dig into the challenges themselves— why it can be so hard for us to step outside our comfort zones in the first place.

The Authenticity Challenge:
"This Isn't Me at All"

I know I am not a real CEO, but rather just some guy running a business.

CEO of a technology company

As Jane Reddy prepared herself to perform her first inspection and interrogation of young cadets at the military academy in the South where she was one of the senior cadets, she started to feel a pit in her stomach. She fully understood the purpose of the daily formation exercises: to make sure that the cadets were prepared and could speak logically under pressure. But the problem was that the aggressive, macho, in-your-face, and often demeaning style with which upperclassmen typically interrogated younger cadets felt deeply uncomfortable and inauthentic to Jane.

Jane's typical style would be *far* less aggressive—but that's not how she was expected to act—or at least how she thought she was expected to act. So when it came time to interrogate her first cadet, and Jane noticed he

25

hadn't shined his belt buckle, which was a requirement for these formation exercises, Jane really let him have it. She screamed like she had never screamed at anyone in her life. She was a drill sergeant on steroids, berating the youngster like nobody's business. And it was successful—so successful, in fact, that after about fifteen seconds, the cadet began to cry.

Now that was not in the plan, and something Jane never expected to happen. There she was, acting like a monster to this poor kid, and the kid starts to cry. And what does Jane do? She starts to scream at him even louder and berate him even more: "You're crying about a belt buckle?? Do you want your mommy?? What's going to happen when you see actual bullets flying??? Are you going to cry then???"

That night, when she went back to the barracks and crawled into bed, exhausted and ashamed, Jane realized that there was no way she could ever do anything like that again. The problem, though, was that she also needed to fit in and perform her role in an effective manner. And she did believe in the ultimate purpose of the activity: to groom upperclassmen as leaders and to test and develop the younger cadets. But the method of doing this was simply intolerable, and she had to figure out a solution . . . and fast. These formations took place daily and she would have to do this same thing all over again to another set of cadets the very next day.

To succeed in today's professional environment, in which we're assuming new roles and responsibilities at a dizzying rate, and the environments themselves are also changing at a rapid pace, in order to catch up we need to reinvent ourselves—often on the fly. And this reinvention sometimes takes the form of learning new behaviors that are necessary but at the same time just don't fit with who we are: As a result, we often end up feeling fake, foreign, or false doing something we know we need to do to be effective or to fulfill our personal or professional responsibilities—but just doesn't feel right or good to be doing. This was certainly the case for Jane Reddy. It was also the case for Jasmit Singh, a fifty-eight-year-old Indian-born senior manager who was recently hired by a young, fast-paced, and entrepreneurial American company to head their logistics division. Previously, Jasmit had been employed for more than twenty years at a Fortune 100 company in the United States, having worked his way up from junior assistant to the VP of operations. But in 2011, Jasmit was laid off following a reorganization and downsizing. He was subsequently hired by

Axiom—a successful and quickly growing start-up in the e-commerce world. On paper it looked like a perfect marriage: Jasmit had just the right background Axiom was looking for, and, on his end, Jasmit felt he was ready for the next challenge in his career. And frankly speaking, he needed another job to pay the bills and maintain his lifestyle. But as soon as he arrived, it became clear that the mix of Jasmit's own personal culture with the Axiom culture was like oil and water.

At the previous company, which had a much more formal and bureaucratic style than the new start-up where he was currently working, Jasmit had achieved such a high level of status that he was often quite insulated from the day-to-day operations of his division. He would receive reports and updates from his senior managers, but it had been years since Jasmit had actually gotten his hands dirty and looked at any of the actual data on his own.

And although he might not readily admit it, the culture of the previous company actually fit pretty well with Jasmit's personal style. Born and raised by strict Indian parents who emphasized deference and politeness in dealing with authority figures, Jasmit was comfortable operating in a strict hierarchy. When he was on the bottom, he was quite deferential and respectful to his superiors, and then at the top, he relished the opportunity to wield his power and authority.

For what it was worth, it also felt natural to him to dress the part of the senior executive. His typical and most comfortable outfit was a suit and tie with matching handkerchief. In fact, one of Jasmit's personal hobbies was collecting high-fashion designer handkerchiefs and pairing them with his designer suits. But Jasmit's style of dress was about two notches more formal than anyone else's at the start-up company, including his boss's—which, of course, wasn't so obvious during the formal interview process but became clear once Jasmit actually started working. While Jasmit wore his trademark suit and handkerchief to the office, pretty much everyone else sported jeans, a polo shirt, and sneakers.

Jasmit also had quite a different style from the rest of the company when it came to delivering presentations. At Axiom, which had a very entrepreneurial, fast-moving culture, everything was extremely practical and to the point. When you delivered a presentation, people wanted data and quick takeaways. They did not want to be lectured, and they certainly didn't want to be delivered "theories" with little practical relevance in the real world. But Jasmit was not like that. Deep down, he truly saw himself as a professor and theorist. It was a core part of his identity and something he was just unwilling—and, frankly, unable—to change. And that's the essence of the authenticity challenge: feeling that the behavior you need to perform to be successful conflicts with who you are at the core.

The Likeability Challenge: "People Won't Like This Version of Me"

> *I think all HR people, at the end of the day,*
> *want to be liked. It is a profession where you*
> *can help people. But no matter how*
> *compassionate you are, they may (still) say,*
> *"What a horrible person that was!"*
>
> **Human resources manager**
> **describing the difficulty of having to do layoffs**

Although it's probably not a surprise to hear that most human beings have a deep and enduring need to be liked, you might not be aware of the extent to which our brains actually crave this positive feedback. Recent studies in neuroscience, for example, have shown that the need to connect socially with others and be liked is as basic as our need for food, water, and shelter. But the problem comes when we need to stretch outside our comfort zones and do something we aren't used to—and, more important, when there's no guarantee that people will actually like us, or this version of ourselves. And that in a nutshell is the likeability challenge.

One particularly vivid example of the likeability challenge can be seen in Annie Jones, the account manager at a private equity firm specializing in high net worth clients. Annie didn't begin her career in sales; after college she worked as a math teacher at an inner-city high school for several years before realizing her hobby of investing in the stock market might be something she could do on a full-time basis. Despite her wariness of taking a job in the macho, male-oriented culture of the financial world, Annie jumped right in with a great job at one of the top firms in Los Angeles.

After only a short time, Annie realized she had made the right decision: The job was a great fit for her. It was fast paced, exciting, and relationship oriented, which played to her strengths, since Annie was quite personable and outgoing. All was good, actually, except for one problem: and that was a very abrasive portfolio manager named Rick Schmitz.

Annie had worked with a few other portfolio managers and had never experienced any problems. But Rick was different. He was your classic asshole—the type of person Bob Sutton writes about in his excellent book *The No Asshole Rule*. Rick made it a point to undermine Annie at every turn—in front of her own boss, with her colleagues, and especially with clients. And because it was firm policy for portfolio managers to accompany account managers on client visits, there was no getting rid of him.

Annie was almost at her breaking point when something happened that brought her over the edge. It happened at the offices of one of the clients Annie had been desperately trying to bring into the firm. As it turned out, the client had concerns about tax issues associated with certain investments—and this was a point that Annie had made to Rick before they went into the room: "Whatever you do, don't ignore or belittle their tax concerns. It could blow the deal." So what did Rick do when they walked into the room? He dismissed the tax concerns—outright. And Annie simply couldn't believe it. In the moment, she desperately tried to smooth over things with the client to save the deal. But inside she was furious. And when she got back to her office, she slammed the door shut and threw all the papers on her desk onto the floor.

Now, when I heard Annie tell this story, I was expecting her to tell me she waltzed right into Rick's office and gave him a piece of her mind. I think anyone would see that as perfectly understandable. But she didn't. And the reason was the exact issue we're discussing here: the likeability challenge. Despite what Rick had done—in this situation and in many others—and despite the fact that Annie would have been justified to throw all the papers off *his* desk instead of hers, she just couldn't pull the trigger. She was so afraid of what Rick would think of her.

You might think this situation is unusual, but I've heard a number of cases just like this, where people avoid communicating information because they're afraid someone will, in their words, "hate" them—even when the possibility is extremely unlikely. Another example comes from Dan Maxwell, a thirty-year-old consultant at a big professional services firm whose version of the likeability challenge arose at the thought of telling his boss that he was leaving the firm. Dan had gotten tired of management consulting and wanted to move on to other things. But he had the hardest time pulling the trigger precisely because of this likeability challenge: Dan was terrified his boss would "hate" him if he left, and as a result he delayed and delayed until at some point he couldn't delay any longer. And guess what? It was a complete nonissue. His boss had no problems with Dan leaving and in fact, confided in Dan that he had been thinking of leaving too.

I have experienced the likeability challenge first-hand, in the case of promoting myself on social media. Initially, I anticipated feeling incompetent at social media—which, as a fortysomething who didn't get a computer until senior year of college, I definitely still am! But really, it was this issue of likeability that ended up being the greatest challenge for me. When I first got into the business of writing books, I never realized that self-promotion and publicity was actually part of the deal. I thought I'd just sit down, write my book, and everyone would then line up to buy it. Well, it's not exactly like that, but I didn't realize I'd have to be the one doing the promoting—of the book and of myself—and when I first started, it felt really uncomfortable. I'd feel a pit in my stomach every time I hit "send" on a tweet or a post, feeling like I was being way too over the top in saying how "great" I was or how "proud" I was about receiving some acknowledgment. I was actually proud—but it's one thing to feel that inside, and another thing entirely to write it and show it to the whole world. I still struggle with this—feeling awkward and uncomfortable tooting my own horn, worrying what people will think of me—but then, ultimately, doing it anyway, or doing my version of it, since I know that it's just part of the deal and if I want to be an author in today's world, it's a "necessary evil."

The Competence Challenge:
"People Can Tell I'm Not Good at This"

My heart is pounding . . . yeah, my heart is definitely pounding, and I am definitely breaking a sweat and, um, my hair is on end on the back of my neck. I don't know, I can't remember exactly, but I'd say it was, you know, definitely an anxiety attack.

—Manager of a Fortune 100 company describing
his experience performing a layoff

Compounding the difficulty of acting outside your comfort zone is the fact that you might also feel incompetent: that you don't have the skills necessary to pull off the task you're trying to perform (and, by the way, that this incompetence is likely visible to others). I remember the deep sense of incompetence I felt when entering a business school classroom for the first time as a professor. I was scared the audience knew more than I did about business (which was probably true). I was scared that I wouldn't get through my material—or that I would finish far too quickly. I also remember the very first time I spoke with executives. I didn't sleep the night before. I woke up bleary-eyed, alternating between drinking coffee to perk up and riding the exercise bike to calm down. I was so insecure about what I was doing and was equally concerned that this was obvious to everyone else in the room.

If you think about it, the competence challenge is such a natural experience when acting outside your comfort zone because, well, when you're learning to act outside your comfort zone, by definition you're doing something you're not familiar with! The competence challenge can be debilitating, not only because of how uncomfortable it feels inside when trying to change your behavior, but also how disconcerting it can be to believe that your incompetence is visible to the world.

Take, for example, the case of Wendy Lodge, who, like Dan Maxwell, was a management consultant at a top professional services firm. When I spoke with Wendy, she was deeply frustrated about the fact that soft skills, such as networking and making small talk, seemed to matter so much at her firm. Wendy remembered vividly how, during her first week at the firm, she saw another new hire—five years younger than she was—chatting informally with the managing director of the firm about the local baseball team. Wendy could never have had that conversation. Not only did she know nothing about baseball, but she also felt awkward trying to make small talk with anyone she did not know well, especially someone as powerful as a managing director. Wendy knew what she had to do. But she felt deeply uncomfortable doing it. She'd try to adapt but it wouldn't go well, and she'd then feel like a failure, which of course made her feel even more uncomfortable—and unwilling—to continue trying to adjust her behavior.

And if this story resonates with you, you should know that it's not just "regular folks" who suffer from the competence challenge. Well-known celebrities are also plagued by feelings of incompetence. Barbra Streisand, for example, experienced such anxiety performing onstage early on in her career that she refused to perform in stadiums and large venues for over twenty-five years. Adele—the Grammy award–winning singer from the UK—was once so scared during a show that she literally fled the stage through a fire exit. Arianna Huffington, founder of the *Huffington Post*, describes this sense of self-doubt as the "obnoxious roommate in our heads," constantly telling us that we can't do something. Actress Reese Witherspoon acutely felt this obnoxious roommate before winning her Oscar for Best Actress for the movie *Walk the Line*, explaining, "I was sitting there hoping they wouldn't call my name—because the idea of having to give a speech in front of everyone in the world is terrifying."

Like other challenges of acting outside your comfort zone, people go to great lengths to hide their anxiety, so much so that when it's revealed, others are often shocked. This was certainly the case for Scott Stossel, the editor of *The Atlantic* magazine, who wrote a deeply personal, poignant book about his own debilitating anxiety and how it has impacted him in a number of different arenas—including public speaking, where he requires a cocktail of antianxiety medication followed by shots of alcohol simply to get himself onstage.

And what can be most debilitating about the competence challenge is what is commonly referred to as the "imposter syndrome"—the fear of being "found out," that your inadequacies will be revealed to the world and you'll be exposed for the fraud that you are. Sounds dramatic, but it's exactly what so many people experience: the feeling that they're posers, imposters, wannabes—and that what they've achieved in life and in business is a fluke just waiting to be exposed. I've definitely experienced this feeling when stepping into a classroom for the first time or, especially now that I'm doing more executive education, walking into a room of fifty managers and executives there to hear me speak. I walk onstage projecting confidence, but inside I feel tremendous doubt that what I have to say to this group of very experienced people will have any value at all.

You might be surprised to hear that imposter syndrome, this variant of the competence challenge, is also pervasive among people who have achieved tremendous accomplishments in life and should seemingly have no doubts about their abilities and competence.

Take, for example, Natalie Portman, the Academy Award–winning actress and Harvard graduate, who returned to Harvard a decade after graduating to deliver a stirring commencement speech about the tremendous self-doubt she experienced during her time at the university. "I felt like there had been some mistake," she said, "that I wasn't smart enough to be in this company, and that every time I opened my mouth I would have to prove that I wasn't just a dumb actress." And it's not just Natalie Portman. So many well-known professionals have suffered, and continue to suffer, from the competence challenge, worrying that they don't have the chops to succeed at tasks outside their comfort zones and that they're going to be found out.

When she won an Oscar for Best Actress for her role in *The Accused*, Jodie Foster thought it must have been a mistake and that she'd have to hand it back: "I thought it was a fluke," she said in an interview with *60 Minutes*. Actor Matt Damon once said that he has "grave concerns about [his own] ability" and that "I just never know if I'm going to pull it off." Sheryl Sandberg, the acclaimed author of *Lean In* and the COO of Facebook, admitted, "I still face situations that I fear are beyond my qualifications. I still have days when I feel like a fraud." Alan Dye, a lead designer at Apple, once said, "I'm scared to death that at some point I'm going to get found out. You know, Tim [Cook] is going to realize the truth about me, which is I'm terrible." And you may also be unaware that, according to a recent survey taken by Roger Jones, chief executive of consulting firm Vantage Hill Partners, the single greatest fear among CEOs is exactly what we've been discussing: incompetence, or what Jones also refers to as imposter syndrome—the idea that you just don't have what it takes to be the final decision-maker in a multibillion-dollar company with hundreds of thousands of people relying on you.

Finally, just to bring home the fact that anyone (really, anyone) can experience the competence challenge—and the imposter syndrome—when facing situations outside their comfort zone. Consider Moses, the great prophet of the Bible (and one of history's first chief executives) who faced down Pharaoh and brought the Israelites out of Egypt. Moses too suffered from imposter syndrome when God told him that he had been selected to speak to Pharaoh and free the Israelites from slavery. He panicked, worried about his capacity to do anything of that sort, especially given his own public speaking challenges. Moses had a speech impediment and was deeply fearful of speaking in public: "I beseech You, O Lord. I am not a man of words, neither from yesterday nor from the day before yesterday, nor from the time You have spoken to Your servant, for I am heavy of mouth and heavy of tongue."

The Resentment Challenge: "Why Do I Have to Do This in the First Place?"

Why do I have to do all this silly, friendly behavior? In my country, if you act like this, you look like a fool.

—Russian-born professional learning
to make small talk in the United States

Even if you *know* you need to adjust your behavior to be effective in a challenging new context, you can still feel resentful about having to do it in the first place. Take, for example, Drew Lyons, an environmental consultant with a phobia of networking events. Now, few of us truly love going to these events where we have to glad-hand potential connections and clients, but for Drew, who was introverted by nature, it was both terrifying and frustrating. Although networking events were key to his business, and Drew knew he had to do them to be successful, he felt deeply resentful that they mattered so much in the first place—even though, of course, he knew logically there was nothing he could do about it.

In some cases, resentment is directed at a person, as in the case of Annie Jones, who was deeply resentful toward her colleague Rick Schmitz's behavior and the fact that she had to expend all this extra effort acting outside her comfort zone in order to confront him. In other cases, the resentment isn't directed at any one person but instead at the general job requirements of a particular position or role.

A good example of this can be found in Roger Evans, a banking executive, who experienced deep levels of resentment when he switched from a large financial firm where he essentially had control over his own projects to a much smaller, consensus-driven firm where he had to work very hard to achieve support for everything he did—even the littlest details . . . and it drove him insane. When we spoke, I could clearly hear the frustration in his voice as he described the situation. Roger was asked to work on improving the new firm's brand—which was stale—in order to compete in a very crowded market-place. So Roger went at it in the only way he knew how, which was to take charge of the project himself—just like he would have done at the previous firm.

And he knocked it out of the park. The new branding was spot-on, and it was going to let the firm finally compete with the top firms in the industry. Job well done, right? Not quite. As it turned out, the self-directed, do-it-yourself process Roger had used to drive the project— which was what he had been taught to use at his old firm—was completely at odds with the deeply collabo-rative culture of the new firm. So much so that when he finished the project and expected a round of high fives, Roger got the cold shoulder. Without realizing it, Roger had completely alienated his colleagues while thinking he was doing a phenomenal job. Roger was livid—at the firm, at his colleagues, and mostly at the fact that he was being punished for something he should have been con-gratulated for.

The Morality Challenge:
"I'm Not Sure I Should Be Doing This"

It's a very uncomfortable feeling. Anyone who tells you that they don't mind laying people off—in my humble opinion—I think is crazy.

—Manager at an apparel company

In most cases, the challenges associated with reaching outside your comfort zone—authenticity, competence, resentment, and likeability in particular—result from this gap in style between how you'd naturally act and how you need to act to be effective. But in some cases, the gap isn't about style; it's about morals: People can have legitimate concerns about the morality of the behavior they're about to perform.

Lily Chang's story from the beginning of the book is a good example of this. Initially, Lily's idea to hire her best friend, Julia, felt like the perfect plan. But that was before Julia bungled two key accounts and caused their website to crash. Julia was a great best friend, but she wasn't a very competent worker. And as the CEO of a start-up working on a shoestring budget, Lily couldn't afford any free riders. Yet despite the fact that Julia had underperformed to a significant degree *and* that her incompetence was threatening the livelihood of the company, Lily had a hard time pulling the trigger on firing her friend, because it just seemed wrong.

A very different example comes from Alan Gosling, who, like Lily, was an entrepreneur building a business. In Alan's case, however, the morality challenge wasn't around firing—it was around hiring. To attract people to his team, Alan had to hide details about his company— such as the fact that the company could go belly-up in a month if key funding didn't come through. There was no legal reason Alan needed to disclose these details; if you think about it, few of us give the whole story when hiring someone into our company. But for Alan, it just still felt deeply uncomfortable being only partially truthful.

I've found evidence of the morality challenge across professions. One of the most poignant examples came from a medical school student at a major metropolitan teaching hospital who was tasked with the job of putting a feeding tube in the stomach of a woman in a coma. According to the student, the woman was in her forties to early fifties and had suffered a stroke. She was thin and didn't have any hair. And even though her prognosis was extremely poor, her family made the decision to start a feeding tube to continue her life. As a result, the medical student was tasked with inserting a feeding tube down the woman's throat—a procedure that was typical for medical students in a teaching hospital to perform, but something this particular student had never done before and felt was deeply troubling. Even though she couldn't say or do or hear anything, the woman clearly was in pain, and the medical student was one of the main people performing this seemingly unnecessary and painful procedure. This is what she wrote about the experience as part of our research project on necessary evils:

> What made me feel even worse, though, was looking at her response to the procedure. She had become completely covered with sweat. There were tears running from her eyes. She struggled against the tube in her throat. She looked frightened and scared. I wondered if she had any idea what was happening to her. If I put myself in her place, it is probably frightening beyond what I can even imagine—to suffer like she has with her illness, now she is unable to communicate her fears or her needs. Is she in pain? Does she want the tube? Does

she even know what is happening to her? The last question troubled me the worst. It must be terrifying to be in a room with a lot of very young-looking people sticking tubes down the throat and cutting holes in the stomach if she doesn't understand what is happening. It sounds like a nightmare.

Finally, one last example of the morality challenge comes from Jessie Wong, who, for years, was a booker on a national morning television program in the United States. A booker's job was to secure guests for the program—and the bigger the news story, the more critical it was to get the scoop, and be first. It was called an "exclusive" in the business, and to do your job well, you had to be able to get them. Now, for many stories, this wasn't much of a morality challenge. For sure it was stressful competing to get these exclusives, but it didn't threaten Jessie's values and beliefs at any core level. That is, except for cases when the news story was a tragedy. And in these situations, the morality challenge was intense.

Imagine, for example, a major plane crash. It was Jessie's job to be the first network to secure interviews with victims' families—even as the tragedy was unfolding. She had to pick up the phone, clench her teeth, tell a mom or dad that she was sorry for their loss but was wondering if they might be willing to come on national TV to talk about it. And each time she did it—each time she heard those cries of raw emotion on the other line—Jessie lost part of her soul. The family members could be crying, even uncontrollably, but you had to do whatever you could to get them on air. And you had to be first.

Few of us are ever going to experience the morality challenge to this degree, but this example highlights the depth of concern people can experience when a task forces them to stretch the boundaries of their morality comfort zone.

All These Emotions Make It Hard to Be Effective

As you can see, acting outside your comfort zone can be a daunting task—whether it comes from a stylistic challenge or a morality challenge, or perhaps even both. People can feel inauthentic, incompetent, resentful, concerned that others won't like this new version of themselves, and worried that what they're doing conflicts with their moral standards.

And the range of emotions that results from these experiences runs the spectrum: from anxiety and distress, to frustration and guilt. Of course people don't necessarily experience all of this in a single situation—although that is certainly possible. But even one or two of these feelings can prove to be disruptive. And you don't need me to tell you what the result can be. Let me just say that it's often not what you'd ideally hope for.

One outcome, for example, is paralysis. You're so utterly overcome with emotion that you simply lose your ability to act or think clearly. In researching this book, I was very surprised to find some examples of exceedingly competent professionals in history who were thrown into paralysis from emotional overload. Actor Hugh Grant once described how panic attacks had overwhelmed him to the point where he nearly quit acting entirely. In his words: "I had all these panic attacks. They're awful. I freeze like a rabbit. Can't speak, can't think, sweating like a bull. When I got home from doing that job, I said to myself, 'No more acting. End of films.'" Another example of paralysis comes from Mahatma Gandhi, who, as a young lawyer, froze from emotional overload while trying a case before a judge, ultimately fleeing the courtroom, humiliated.

No one likes to feel overwhelmed—and certainly no one likes to have their emotions spill over in a way that's potentially even humiliating for them. And yet, that's what can happen when acting outside your comfort zone. In my work, I've seen many cases of people rendered completely incompetent by emotion—often at the most critical moments of their job. One such story occurred at a Fortune 500 company where a very senior director at the firm froze right in the middle of telling a longtime employee he was losing his job. The senior director in question, Carl, had to fire one of his longtime managers—someone he knew exceedingly well. The company—as many companies do—had developed a script to help managers deliver the news in a clear, direct, and compassionate manner. An HR manager brought Carl a copy of the script to practice with. Supremely confident in his abilities, Carl rejected the script and told the HR manager he "got it." But when the employee walked into the room for the meeting—and realized he was about to be fired—Carl became flooded with emotion and froze. And instead of delivering the message as intended, he clutched the script in his shaking hand and literally started reading from it—like a robot delivering the message.

In Carl's case, emotional overload led to paralysis, but that's not always the case. In other situations, people "unload" their emotion—yelling, screaming, or even using violence. For example, one manager in our research about necessary evils described how for her, emotion was a hot potato that she had to get rid of at all costs, even if it meant a far less compassionate delivery of the message: "You deliver the message in this kind of hurried panic way: 'There, I said it. I got it out. I freed myself of the burden of that news and now it is yours.' They just look at you and burst into tears. Then you feel totally helpless to assist them."

In yet other cases, emotional overload results in tears. For people brought to tears, the effect is often so powerful that there's nothing you can do about it. I found the following story from the *Huffington Post* quite poignant and illustrative of this effect. In the story, the author describes a deeply frustrating experience trying to confront her son's day-care supervisor about concerns she had about the care her son was receiving. She's simply overcome by emotion and starts to cry: "I am thirty seconds into a discussion with an administrator at my son's day care, when I feel it coming. I have asked her to watch out for another boy who has been biting my son, but she brushes off my concerns. 'It's just a phase,' she tells me. 'It will stop. Besides, the boy who bites is much smaller than your son.' In that moment, when I feel ignored, dismissed, infuriated . . . my cheeks flush, and I start to cry."

In my research, I've actually found crying to be a more frequent reaction than you'd imagine. People are often afraid to step outside their comfort zones because they know they'll cry—or they fear they'll cry. And sometimes it just comes out, uncontrollably. For example, that was the case for a VP of human resources at a Fortune 500 company. After feeling slighted at a meeting with her director, she rushed into her immediate supervisor's office and burst into tears. In this instance, the slight wasn't a random occurrence; it was a set of feelings built up over time after having felt slighted a number of times and never having had the courage to confront her director about her feelings.

The examples you have just read were fairly intense reactions to having to act outside your comfort zone. But emotions don't necessarily have to be that intense to be disruptive. I know cases where the emotions people experience when confronted with a situation outside their comfort zones are just disruptive or uncomfortable enough to tilt their mind-set from "approach" to "avoid"—from being willing to take a shot at handling an uncomfortable situation to finding anything they can possibly do to avoid it. And this amazing capacity we all have to avoid situations outside our comfort zones is exactly what we're going to focus on next.

CHAPTER 2

Our Amazing Capacity to Avoid

Avoiding situations and tasks that frighten us is, in many ways, the most natural thing in the world. Evolutionarily speaking, it has also probably helped our species to survive! We see a bear and run from the bear. We see a lion and run from the lion. The problem comes when you apply this very same fight-or-flight reaction to situations that *aren't* genuinely life-threatening—like taking on a new role at work, for example. When we avoid these sorts of tasks, we get the temporary relief from anxiety and fear, but we also limit real opportunities that put us outside our comfort zones but could also be compelling and meaningful—such as developing new skills.

With that in mind, I've uncovered an array of impressive tactics we all use to avoid situations outside our comfort zones. As you go through them, think to yourself if any of these avoidance tactics applies to you.

Tactic #1: Full-On Avoidance

All of us in one way or another construct our lives at home and at work to avoid things that cause discomfort. Warren Buffett once lamented that in college he limited himself by only signing up for classes where he wouldn't have to put himself out on a limb and speak in public. And whenever he did have to speak in public, especially in the early days, the results weren't pretty: "I would throw up," Buffett remarked. "In fact, I arranged my life so that I never had to get up in front of anybody." The famous classical composer Frédéric Chopin was so uncomfortable performing in public that he turned down countless opportunities, performing only forty or so times in public in his thirty-year career.

And of course, it's not just speaking in public that people fear. Many people avoid casual get-togethers at work because of their fear of making unscripted small talk with colleagues. In a recent survey commissioned by Age UK as part of a campaign to combat loneliness in the United Kingdom, researchers found that 60 percent of British people preferred being by themselves instead of making small talk by the watercooler. The study also provided some very interesting insight into the techniques people use to avoid human contact, including hiding behind computer screens, making fake phone calls, and feigning deafness.

Of course, there are some tasks and situations that you simply can't avoid doing: for example, most professors can't avoid teaching, even if they wanted to, because teaching is an inherent feature of the job. However, professors do have more leeway to avoid things like presenting at conferences or giving keynote speeches to corporate audiences. Oftentimes, the more power you have in an organization, the better equipped you are to structure your work life to avoid stressful tasks, because you're less accountable to, say, a manager or supervisor looking over your shoulder. For a very senior person, the stakes are often higher, since many people assume that people in top leadership positions should be capable of doing things such as giving speeches or delivering bad news—even if this is not necessarily true. As a case in point, consider this description from Alexander Stein of *Fortune Small Business* of a CEO of a small company who was so terrified of asking customers and clients to pay invoices in a timely manner that he avoided the task altogether—obviously to the detriment of his own business: "[The CEO] understood what steps he needed to take to fix his business: Collect late receivables, trim expenses, and negotiate larger upfront retainers from new clients. But he was paralyzed by the mere prospect of pressing customers to pay those overdue invoices. Actually make the call? Impossible. The mere thought of asking a client for more money made him feel like Albert Brooks's sweaty, hyperventilating character in *Broadcast News*."

Tactic #2: Do the Task, but Only Partway—and Not So Well

Pure avoidance isn't always possible, and that's why people sometimes opt to do the task, but only partway. For example, instead of going to a business dinner to meet key potential clients, you post details of your business on social media. Rather than giving a motivational speech to employees, you decide to send an inspirational message via Facebook. Or instead of meeting new people at a networking event, you sit at the bar with the people you came with, or you spend lots of time in the drink line or in the bathroom—anything to kill time and avoid the possibility of having to talk with a stranger. When you go back to the office you can "check the box" that says you attended a networking event, but you didn't speak to a single person you didn't know.

Someone I spoke with who engaged in this avoidance tactic was Dan Gold, a car wash entrepreneur whose real claim to fame was a unique system of software he had developed to run car washes more efficiently. Dan loved developing the software and didn't avoid that at all. But when it came down to sales—actually asking a potential customer to purchase the product—his real avoidance behavior kicked in. Dan truly believed in the product— and from running it in his own car wash, he knew it worked. But he hated to impose. He dreaded the idea of actually looking someone in the eye and asking them for thousands of dollars.

Logically, he knew the software was perfectly sensible and legitimate. His system would save the client thousands of dollars in the first year, essentially paying for itself. But the client didn't know that, and every time he started to ask for a purchase, he clammed up and avoided the situation. It was a lot like seeing a pretty woman, chatting with her, getting the sense she might actually be attracted to you as well, and then just saying nothing. And to top it off, when clients came to him, essentially begging him to sell them the product, Dan would sell it to them at a discount—afraid again of imposing on them, even though they were the ones coming to him. In the end, Dan did get his software business off the ground, but much slower than he had hoped to. And it was all due to the fears he experienced stepping outside his comfort zone and the avoidance behavior that ensued.

In our work on necessary evils, I have seen many cases of people performing challenging tasks only partway. A particularly memorable example comes from research by Larry Stybel and his colleagues on executive dismissals. In their example, a president of a company tried to cushion the blow when firing a sales executive at his firm, saying that the employee was "too high powered" for the job, and telling him, "We've got to look into getting you a better match between your high abilities and a reasonable job" without actually saying that he was being let go. And, not surprisingly, delivering the news only partway in this circumstance did not result in a positive outcome, as the sales executive didn't actually realize he was being fired.

Tactic #3: Procrastinate

A perfect way to avoid tasks outside our comfort zones is to delay doing them. We all do it—telling ourselves that we'll start writing that report when the dishes are done . . . and then when the news is over . . . and then when the kids are asleep . . . and then when the television program is over . . . We procrastinate at home and at work; in fact, a recent survey suggests that 95 percent of us procrastinate at least occasionally and 25 percent of us admit to doing it consistently and problematically. And among this procrastinating group, apparently, are some famous figures: Bill Clinton is known to be a chronic procrastinator. According to *Time* magazine, Clinton would wait weeks before commenting on drafts of speeches, until the very last minute. Al Gore called him "punctually challenged," and Hillary Clinton said that it was "maddening to keep him on any kind of schedule." Many historical figures have struggled with procrastination as well. Author Herman Melville report-edly had his wife chain him to his desk to avoid procras-tination when he was writing *Moby-Dick*.

A poignant example of procrastination from my re-search comes from Neil Kennedy, the entrepreneur who had created a Facebook-like site years before Facebook was ever launched. Neil was poised to create riches for himself and his investors—but he had one problem: pro-crastination. Neil felt much more comfortable and safe in "tinkering mode," perfecting every last bell and whis-tle before introducing it to the general public. In the end, Neil's procrastination—and reluctance to expose his ideas to scrutiny—let others catch up and overtake him. And the rest is history.

Although almost all of us procrastinate, few of us admit that we do. Instead, we create excuses for our behavior—stories we tell ourselves about why we're doing something that is really procrastination in dis-guise. Neil's disguise, for instance, was about "being careful"; in other words, by tinkering for so long, he was simply being a thoughtful and careful CEO. Another ex-cuse might be looking for the "perfect" timing, as in: the perfect time to launch a website or make a career move, or, in Lily Chang's case, fire her best friend.

Tactic #4: Pass the Buck

If all else fails, another popular task-avoiding strategy is to "pass the buck": have someone else perform a task that you should be doing. For example, if you're a business owner and afraid of networking, you might send your assistant to network, even though you should be the one to represent your company. Or if you're a CEO who is fearful of public speaking, you might have someone else deliver a motivational speech, even if it would be more appropriate if the speech came from you. Buck passing is especially pervasive around delivering bad news, which people are commonly fearful of delivering.

In one particularly striking case of passing the buck, an employee at a New Jersey chemical company sabotaged the company's computer system to the tune of twenty million dollars in damage, precisely because of this issue of buck passing, which is evident in a note he wrote to the president of the company:

I have been loyal to the company in good and bad times for over thirty years. I was expecting a

*member of top management to come down from
his ivory tower to face us with the layoff announce-
ment rather than sending the kitchen supervisor
with guards to escort us off the premises like crim-
inals. You will pay for your senseless behavior.*

Another case of buck passing comes from a survey
conducted by consulting company Development Dimensions International (DDI) and the Economist Intel-
ligence Unit of 420 worldwide executives that found six
out of ten leaders were worried that their organizations
weren't developing talented employees quickly enough
to compete . . . but at the same time, these leaders seemingly weren't willing to get their hands dirty and be sig-
nificantly involved in the development process itself.
Only 20 percent of the executives admitted to actually
spending time helping to develop talent, and only 10
percent had reviewed the issue with their boards. As
Matt Paese, one of the survey project leaders, noted: "It's
astounding given the fact that they recognize the business impact of having the right people—yet they're outsourcing accountability for it."

A Vicious Cycle of Avoidance

As we've seen, stepping outside our comfort zones in a meaningful and consequential professional situation can be very challenging to do—and for a variety of reasons. We can feel disingenuous and inauthentic acting in a way that's against the grain of our own personalities. We can feel awkward, self-conscious, and sometimes even inappropriate trying on a set of behaviors that just doesn't fit quite right. And we can also sometimes even feel resentful that we have to go through all these conniptions in the first place, wondering why "just being ourselves" isn't enough to get us where we want to go. Furthermore, because of these feelings, we often do whatever we can to reduce that anxiety, usually to our detriment.

Imagine you're afraid of snakes, and because of this fear you keep your distance. Each time you see a snake, you flee, protecting yourself in the short term, but never actually confronting your fear. And each time, by avoiding the snake, the fear grows stronger, since you're that much further removed from any sort of realistic appraisal of encountering a snake—which, if you were willing to try, might teach you that it's not so scary after all. But you avoid and avoid, and each time you avoid, the chances of ever confronting the snake get smaller and smaller.

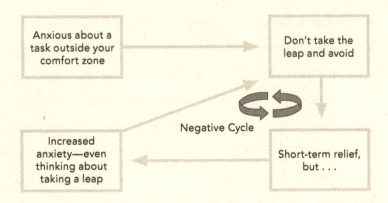

Vicious Cycle of Avoidance

You can see the idea: You continue to avoid, the fear continues to grow, and you become phobic of snakes, arranging your life to do what you can to avoid them. Now, of course with snakes, this isn't necessarily a bad thing, but when your "snake" is making small talk . . . or talking to your boss . . . or giving negative feedback . . . or giving positive feedback—that's where avoidance becomes dysfunctional. You start constructing your work life to avoid tasks that are really important to your chances of personal and professional success. And that is the paradox of avoidance: By avoiding stressful situations, you actually end up increasing your level of stress over time. You can see this clearly on the diagram on p. 66.

Starting in the box in the upper left, if you are anxious about a task outside your comfort zone, you do whatever you can—probably using one of the tactics we just discussed—to avoid taking the leap. And what's particularly nice about the strategy of avoidance is that it pays immediate dividends: You don't actually have to do the stressful task! You have found a way around it. That's the benefit in the short term. But over time, as you encounter additional opportunities to do the task, your anxiety increases—since the task now almost has a taboo quality to it—it's not only stressful, but it's also something you're actively avoiding. That, then, of course ups the ante to ever take the leap and try it—which becomes increasingly unlikely, and you increase avoidance over time, perpetuating the negative cycle pictured in the diagram: not taking the leap, feeling short-term relief, and then avoiding again.

PART II

How to Successfully
Reach Outside
Your Comfort Zone

You'd like to contribute to discussions at your company but can never get yourself to jump into the fray. You know you need to network, but you feel uneasy starting conversations with strangers. You need to start emphasizing your professional accomplishments at work to be noticed, but you feel deeply uncomfortable about tooting your own horn. This list of uncomfortable but necessary tasks that all of us face at work could go on and on. And with the constant change in our lives and in our organizations, it's only going to get more challenging. We're crossing national cultures and organizational cultures on a regular basis; we're moving from one functional culture to another and also changing professional cultures often. We're changing roles—from editor to agent, from product developer to CEO, from nurse to nurse manager—and we're even switching careers. And with each of these changes comes a "stretch" in our roles and responsibilities that forces us out of our comfort zones and challenges our skills and personalities.

The problem, of course, is that acting outside our comfort zones can be incredibly challenging, as the previous section of the book just illustrated. People pleasers often dread delivering bad news, sometimes avoiding the task altogether because of how uncomfortable it feels. Introverts can struggle having to schmooze, work a room, or pitch their products. And it can be terrifying for anyone with a fear of speaking in public to step up to the platform to deliver a speech. But this is the reality at work for most of us: As we grow and learn and advance in our jobs and in our careers, we're constantly faced with situations outside our comfort zones where we need to adapt and adjust our behavioral styles. And without the ability—and courage—to step outside our comfort zones and learn to stretch and flex our behavior, it's very difficult to be successful.

The goal of this next section of the book is to give you the insight and perspective that you need to take the leap and act outside your own personal comfort zone, in whatever type of situation you face. And that initial leap does not have to be a big one. It fact, it probably shouldn't be. If you're afraid of giving a speech in front of thousands of people, start by giving a speech to a few friends, or to a small group of people from your unit or department, or sign up for a public speaking organization like Toastmasters. Or if you're terrified of networking, don't begin with the most challenging environment imaginable. Start in the break room with colleagues, or perhaps at an alumni event where you know a few people.

When reaching beyond our comfort zones, we all need support—what the Russian psychologist Lev Vygotsky calls "scaffolding." And so the goal of this next section is to offer you the best scaffolding I know, which comes to you in the form of three critical resources for behavior flexing: tools that provide you with the confidence, courage, and capability to take that leap and truly commit to acting outside your comfort zone. These resources are: 1) conviction: having a deep sense of purpose in what you're doing and why; 2) customization: finding your own personal way of performing the task so it feels as natural as possible to you; and 3) clarity: the ability to gain perspective on the challenges you face and how you might be avoiding the situation. In the next few chapters, we'll examine each of these key resources and how you can incorporate them into your own personal repertoire.

CHAPTER 3

Conviction: The Critical Importance of Having a Deep Sense of Purpose

As she meandered her way through traffic to her new office in downtown Washington, DC, Lisa Warren nearly took a turn right off the freeway to her home in the suburbs. It was the first day of work in her new job as head of research at a small but fairly prominent think tank—and she felt way out of her league. Lisa was smart—there was no doubt about that. She was an Ivy League grad, had worked at a very well-known consulting firm, and had just finished a master's program at one of the top public policy schools in the country. But she was stepping into a new job where she felt like a total imposter. She was going to be the head of research and development for the entire organization—with no management experience, little previous research experience, and no PhD, which was the typical degree for the head of research.

And then there was the issue of her age. Lisa was twenty-eight and the rest of the senior staff was at least fifteen years older than her—and, in fact, the person she was replacing was a fifty-five-year-old with a PhD. Lisa felt like a poser and, frankly, wondered whether they somehow got it all wrong when they hired her. She did have a few in-person interviews—so they must have known who she was. But she kept having these fantasies that they had hired the wrong Lisa Warren. After all, it wasn't that uncommon a name. Perhaps there was another Lisa Warren who was much more qualified than she was, but by mistake they sent the job offer and email to her.

And because of all this—the worry, the feelings of ineptitude, the fear . . . it felt so awful to walk into this job feeling so unprepared and unqualified—and she nearly didn't even do it. That turn off the freeway back home had never felt so tempting. But in the end, Lisa did stay in her lane, got off the proper exit to work, and started at the new job. And what motivated her to "approach" when every bone in her body was saying "avoid" is exactly what I'd like to talk about right now: I call it conviction.

If there were no justifiable reason to act outside your comfort zone—if networking really weren't all that important to your career . . . if making small talk with colleagues didn't matter at all . . . and if asserting yourself were truly irrelevant to your job, acting outside your comfort zone would be a moot point. You'd laugh at the idea of doing any of these things because the "gain" clearly isn't worth the "pain" it takes to do them. But of course, if you've picked up this book, there must be something outside your comfort zone you'd like to get better at. And that's where the power of conviction comes in. Conviction is a deep belief in the purpose of what you're doing—that this purpose is legitimate and valid and worth enduring strain or stress to achieve. It's what the great American pastor Harry Emerson Fosdick meant when he said: "[People] will work hard for money. They will work harder for other [people]. But [people] will work hardest of all when they are dedicated to a cause."

And that's exactly what enabled Lisa to give the job a

go. Environmental studies and corporate social responsibility was in her blood. She deeply cared about it. She was an environmental studies major in college, had interned at the Sierra Club, and had focused her studies on these same issues during her master's program, culminating with a hands-on final project helping local firms become more socially responsible citizens. The new job was scary, no doubt, but in Lisa's words, it was "scary-exciting." Despite her feeling ill prepared to handle the job she had been given, she still felt a deep connection with the purpose. And that helped her fight through the discomfort she had.

Purpose Has Many Sources

Conviction can come from many sources. In some cases, it comes from improving your own lot in life. For example, by performing a particularly challenging task, you can enhance your reputation, accelerate your own skill development, or boost your self-esteem. For Barbara Corcoran, the New York real estate tycoon, the conviction to step outside her comfort zone—which, in her case, meant being a regular on the ABC television show *Shark Tank*—came from wanting to feel that she belongs, especially in a group of mostly men: "When I first started the show, inside I was frightened to death." But she overcame this fear by having conviction that "I have a right to be here."

People are also sometimes inspired to step outside their comfort zones to help others. Take, for example, fund-raising, which many people feel to be a particularly distasteful and challenging task. In one research study, Adam Grant of the Wharton School showed how simply giving fund-raisers conviction about what they're doing—which, in this case, entailed meeting someone who received a scholarship as a result of their efforts—dramatically changed their experience of the task. Having conviction also impacted how persistent the callers were and how much they ended up raising for future scholarship recipients. As it turned out, the callers who had interacted with the scholarship student—for a mere five minutes—spent more than twice as long on the phone and raised nearly three times the money, due in large part to the power of conviction and, in particular, the power of wanting to contribute to something greater than themselves.

Another interesting demonstration of the power of "externally" focused conviction comes from organizational psychologists Emily Amanatullah of the University of Texas and Michael W. Morris of Columbia University, who showed that women are far more successful at being assertive during a negotiation when they are advocating for a friend or mentee instead of for themselves. When the women negotiated for themselves, they asked for an average of $7,000 less than men did doing the same task. But when the women negotiated on behalf of a friend, they asked for just as much money as the men. So, again, in this case, having a clear purpose of the "gain" for the pain you're enduring makes you much more successful, both at coping with the pain and at realizing the gain.

In the research we did with managers, police officers, addiction counselors, and doctors performing "necessary evils" at work, we found a similar effect of conviction as in the studies above: Having a deep sense of the purpose of your actions—of being able to improve your own lot in life or the circumstances for someone else—enabled professionals in the settings we studied to perform tasks such as painful medical procedures, layoffs, and evictions that, were it not for this underlying purpose, would be extremely difficult to perform. Police officers, for example, found conviction to be an essential psychological resource to help them keep their own sanity when evicting people from their homes. I actually witnessed this firsthand when I did a "ride-along" with two officers on their daily run of twenty evictions. And during this ride-along, with bulletproof vest and all (many of their evictions are in the very worst parts of the city), I realized how, as was the case with the other professional groups, conviction was a critical resource for these officers, a buffer against the internal struggle they felt when stepping into someone's home and telling them that they have to leave, often immediately. The officers I got to know explained how important it was for them to uphold the law and do their job despite having to evict tenants who were truly down on their luck. And then, in cases of rent evaders—and there were definitely some of those as well—the officers talked about the importance of supporting landlords, who were losing tens of thousands of dollars from these "deadbeat" tenants.

Conviction served a similar purpose for the addiction counselors we studied who sometimes had to terminate clients from their rehabilitation facility for bad behavior, despite the fact that there would be a much greater chance of relapse on the outside. I remember one particularly difficult case in an addiction facility that we studied, where a longtime counselor there had to terminate a client because he had broken too many rules to remain. The philosophy of the facility was to teach people responsibility by setting clear rules and enforcing violations of the rules in a consistent manner. So terminating a client who had violated too many rules was perfectly aligned with the center's philosophy. It was still, however, quite difficult to do—and that's where the sense of purpose came in. It was painful, it was difficult, it caused the counselor to lose sleep at night—but it was something that simply had to be done.

Pediatric physicians echoed a similar theme: using conviction as an antidote to the discomfort that they experienced when performing painful procedures on children. As one physician explained: "I never liked the feeling of hearing a kid's cry, but the more I'm convinced that it really needs to be done, the better I feel about it."

Not surprisingly, conviction was also a critical resource for many of the characters you've already read about in this book. Remember Annie Jones, the account manager at an equity firm for high net worth clients who was being undermined during client meetings by her obnoxious colleague Rick Schmitz? Annie was terrified that she'd come across as a whiner and complainer, and on top of it, she was afraid she might actually break down emotionally while delivering the message, which of course would make things that much more humiliating. In the end, Annie did confront Rick—and was actually quite successful. Annie knew that if she wanted to succeed at her job—especially in a male-dominated industry like finance—she *had* to learn to stand up for herself. It was absolutely critical and she had no other choice. But she also boosted this sense of conviction by recognizing over time that the behavior wasn't just necessary but also legitimate and justifiable. This piece took a bit longer, because deep down Annie didn't really think it was okay to be assertive like this. Annie hadn't been raised to be confrontational—in fact, quite the opposite. She grew up in a strict, religious Catholic family, where you were taught to speak only when spoken to. That background, combined with her timid nature, made it feel wrong to tell her colleague off—at least initially.

But that perspective changed too over time. Annie realized that telling Rick off wasn't just a way for Annie to vent her frustration; it was also a way to communicate to Rick the effect that his actions were having on her and on the business. And after all, if Annie didn't have the courage to point out to Rick the effect his behavior was having on her, she really had no one to blame but herself. All this is a way of saying that Annie came to a series of epiphanies that stepping outside her comfort zone was critical for her to do her job—and that it was perfectly acceptable behavior. In the end, these two sources of conviction—that standing up for herself was both necessary and justifiable—were what pushed her over the hump. Ultimately, Annie deserved better treatment, and recognizing that became a very powerful motivator for her.

Lily Chang also used conviction as a resource for mustering up the courage to take on a very challenging task, which, in her case, was firing her best friend. Ultimately, what tilted Lily's perspective was the other people involved who depended on the success of the business. Like the women in the negotiation study I referenced earlier who had an easier time negotiating on behalf of someone else, Lily made a point to think of all the people aside from her who were being impacted by Julia's incompetence . . . and there were many of them. For example, to start the firm, Lily had borrowed money from her parents and relatives—and that was money she had to repay from future profits from the firm. Lily was also indebted to venture capitalists who invested in the company and then most importantly to her employees— many of whom had left high-paying jobs to bet on Lily and the promise of her company. And she couldn't let these people down—any of them. So, although the task of firing her best friend was incredibly difficult, having a deep sense of conviction about the justifiability of doing so—as well as the necessity to do it—made a very difficult task that much more palatable.

Best-selling author and Wharton professor Adam Grant wrote in a recent LinkedIn post about how he had experienced a very similar transformation around public speaking—which, for Adam, is a fear he's had to overcome in his professional life. Here's what Adam wrote about his initial experiences of speaking in public:

"Several years ago, I was invited to give my first public speech, and I made the mistake of saying yes. I was terrified: As a student, my heart used to race at the mere thought of raising my hand in class. For weeks beforehand, I had nightmares about forgetting my lines, waking up in a cold sweat. No matter how much I practiced, for the three days leading up to the speech, I could hardly breathe."

Interestingly, like Annie, Lily, Roger, and many others, Adam too seemed to have come to a richer and deeper sense of why public speaking matters to him, which serves as a powerful source of conviction when worry sets in. He wrote: "When I feel pangs of panic about speaking, I no longer try to fight the reasons to stop. I focus on the reasons to go: I'm delivering a message that matters deeply to me. I enjoy challenging assumptions, offering actionable insights, and providing some entertainment. As my enthusiasm climbs, anxiety fades."

Finally, in certain cases, conviction comes not only from a belief in the underlying purpose of your actions but also from a deep sense of calling within yourself. That was definitely the case for Reverend Barbara Harris, an Episcopal priest I interviewed about the challenges of acting outside her comfort zone. In her case, this meant visiting dying family members in the hospital and potentially giving them last rites. Although we may sometimes forget, behind every priest, cleric, reverend, or rabbi is a human being—a human being with insecurities and fears about being able to pull off very important tasks outside their comfort zones. That was definitely the case for Barbara. She'd be playing with her children or cooking dinner and that phone call would come in: "Reverend, I'm sorry to bother you, but I was wondering if you might be able to come visit the hospital. My relative is dying and there isn't much time left." She'd drop whatever she was doing and go right over.

For Barbara, the greatest challenge wasn't necessarily the lack of warning, or even the fact that the situation was so unscripted and unpredictable—although those aspects of the job were certainly challenging. Instead, it was the enormity of the situation that was so overwhelming. Another human being is dying, a family is grieving, and then there's you. You desperately want to do the right thing—to handle the situation with grace and courage. And as you walk up the stairs and turn that doorknob, not knowing what to expect, you feel this deep sense of existential angst: "Who am I to be doing this? What right do I have to be performing this enormous task?" Of course, the answer is: You're a priest and this is your job. But at a deeper level, you're also a human being. And the task just seems larger than life.

That's exactly where conviction comes into play, at least for Barbara. In that moment—that larger-than-life moment—what grounds Barbara is the very deep sense of conviction she has in her calling and in God. God has put her on earth to play this role and so that's what she has to do. And, in fact, she's not alone because God is right there with her. As she turns the knob, walks into the room, and fumbles with her prayer book, she prays deep inside herself to God, and God works through her to provide the grace and courage to be successful.

CHAPTER 4

Customization:
Finding Your Own Personal
Way of Performing the Task

Lucy Wong was in the zone: She was finishing the tail end of a report that was supposed to be due on Friday—three days from then—and was probably going to finish everything else she needed to get done for the week by the next day. And this wasn't something new. Lucy was a prodigy—that's what brought her from a small town in Wyoming to Yale University and then Harvard Business School and now to Bain and Company,

where she was a junior associate hoping, like everyone else, to make the grade and be promoted to senior
associate—which, for Lucy, was a dream ever since she
started at the firm. As one of the top management consulting firms in the industry, Bain was full of prodigies,
but there were few as incredibly capable as Lucy. She was
a crackerjack econometrician, having graduated summa
cum laude in three years from Yale with a dual degree in
math and economics. And to top it off, Lucy was also
fluent in three languages: English from growing up in
the States; Mandarin, which she spoke at home with her
parents; and German, from going to a German-American
high school, which her parents thought would give her
a leg up as she embarked on her business career.

Lucy had everything going for her except for one
thing (and it was actually a pretty big thing): She was
terrified of speaking up in meetings. You see, Lucy had
grown up in a fairly strict Chinese household where she
was taught to respect hierarchy and to speak when spoken to. That, combined with her naturally shy and introverted personality, made it very hard for her to speak her
mind—initially at school (where even as early as fourth
grade her teachers praised her ability but hoped she'd
become more outspoken over time) and then in college
and beyond. Now, if Lucy were in a profession like aca-

demics, which was what both her parents did—this personality might have been a great fit. She could lock herself in her office, crank out brilliant papers, and achieve the success she desired.

But in management consulting, you really had to put yourself out there. You had to participate actively in meetings—especially as a young consultant—to establish your reputation. You had to have a point of view (a hypothesis) and you needed to challenge others' points of view and hypotheses, often in vigorous brainstorming-style discussions. And—this was the worst of it—these conversations often involved senior members of the firm. So Lucy, who was terrified of even calling a partner by her first name, had to pitch and promote and defend her ideas in public, potentially even critiquing others' ideas—right there in front of senior members of the firm! That was so far outside Lucy's comfort zone that she almost quit the firm because of it. But she did genuinely love the work, and, quite honestly, couldn't quit—at least not yet—because of the blow it would be to her entire family, who were so proud of what she had achieved.

Lucy ended up being quite successful, despite the significant gaps that she experienced between her preferred quiet, modest, self-effacing style and the far more assertive, direct style she needed in order to succeed at Bain. What's particularly interesting and relevant to this chapter is *how* she was able to achieve this success. Now, conviction was certainly part of the story: Lucy cared deeply about succeeding at Bain, and for many reasons—including her own sense of pride and accomplishment as well as the way that success would impact her family. But it wasn't just this sense of conviction that enabled her to succeed—it was the combination of conviction and what I like to call "customization"—or putting your own personal touch or spin on behaviors you're trying to master.

If you think about it, we really live in an era of customization. We personalize and customize our logos and our lattes. We customize our coats, our jeans, even our books. We customize our computers, our iPhones, and our iPads. And while working on our customized computers, we can munch on customized M&M's and muesli. When it comes to consumer goods, we no longer live in a one-size-fits-all world. And the same is true for adapting and adjusting our behavior. For example, in Lucy's case, there wasn't one single way for her to succeed at Bain. There was a general set of expectations— that you needed to get your voice heard at meetings, for instance, or that you need to have opinions and share them with confidence—and the trick is to find your way to achieve those goals. That's customization of behavior and it was exactly what Lucy did to achieve success at Bain and learn to stretch beyond her comfort zone.

One tool Lucy used was the customization of her words. When she started working at Bain, she noticed that to command the respect of others she had to be able to point out the flaws in their ideas—often during brainstorming discussions with multiple partners in the room. Initially Lucy was floored by how confident many junior consultants sounded when doing this—saying things like "I don't buy that" when pointing out the weaknesses in an argument. They often were right, but that language just sounded incredibly assertive and direct to Lucy, far outside her comfort zone.

But what Lucy discovered was that she could actually feel comfortable doing this if she made just a few subtle word choices that suited her more than "I don't buy that"—which just made her cringe. So, instead Lucy would say something like "Huh, that's interesting. Can you tell me more about why you believe that?" It essentially achieved the same effect as the more assertive version—and, in fact, was still a stretch for Lucy to make. But it didn't feel so deeply inauthentic, and thus had much more staying power.

Another customization tool Lucy applied was the use of a room's seating arrangement to her advantage. She would consistently sit next to people who were of higher power, especially if they were clients, because she had noticed that when they had questions, they'd often turn to the person next to them—even if it was a junior consultant—to help explain. And Lucy realized that by merely positioning herself next to them, she could get to be that person—the one to explain a complicated idea to the client—and, as it turned out, look positive in the eyes of the client as well as the people from her firm who observed the situation.

Lucy customized this situation in other ways too: She often volunteered to be the "scribe" for the meeting, which let her stand instead of sit, and also to be in front of the room, controlling what made it onto the whiteboard. Although this was subtle, it too enabled her to both appear and feel more powerful. There was something about being at the front of the room—especially as a junior consultant, pacing around a table of senior colleagues with a pen in her hand—that actually made her feel powerful.

So, Lucy did get promoted—and in large part due to the clever ways that she was able to customize her experience.

The Many Tools of Customization

When I speak about customization, I like to use a variety of metaphors to bring the idea to life. The first is the metaphor of a tailor. Imagine going to a local department store and picking up a new pair of pants or a new suit. Now, there are those lucky few of us who are able to walk right up to a rack, say "I'll take that one," and have it fit like a glove. But for the rest of us (me included, by the way), we need to tweak and customize the clothing so it fits just right. Remember that the clothing in question wasn't made for you, but you can customize it so it can feel like it was. And as you'll see in a moment, you can do the very same thing with the situations that you feel are outside your comfort zone—in life and at work. You can make alterations to these situations, often very slight ones and, as is the case with clothing, alterations that others might be completely oblivious to, but that make you feel more comfortable, competent, and capable.

Another example that I think is particularly useful for capturing this notion of customization is acting. When actors are assigned a role, most of the time that role isn't 100 percent ironclad complete. There's typically a bit of wiggle room to adjust the role so that it fits just right. That means perhaps trimming a bit of behavior that may not be critical to the part and that feels particularly inauthentic to you. It might also mean adding something that, again, doesn't change the role in any major way but makes you feel more comfortable and confident enacting it. It might mean tweaking your verbal behavior or your nonverbal behavior; it might involve introducing props or playing with the timing of the role; and, in some cases, it might even involve introducing other characters. And this happens to be the exact same set of tools that all of us can use to customize our roles in life—to make them feel more authentic, to reduce anxiety and distress, and to increase our level of competence and confidence, especially when we're trying to grow and develop and stretch beyond our comfort zones.

What's particularly nice about customization is that it puts the power back in our court. Often, when facing difficult situations outside our comfort zones, we feel powerless. However, knowing that we have the power to tweak and adjust and alter the situation to our liking—within reasonable limits—is quite an empowering idea. So, with Lucy as inspiration, let's take a look at the tools at our disposal: how we can sculpt situations in a way that plays to our strengths; redefines our roles to decrease anxiety, increases authenticity, and effectiveness; and brings us that much closer to success outside our comfort zone.

CUSTOMIZE THE WORDS YOU USE

As you saw in the case of Lucy Wong, one of the simplest but most powerful ways to play to our strengths is by customizing our dialogue—that is, what we actually say.

There are many ways you can customize language to your advantage. Imagine you find out that your employees don't appreciate the fact that you're not praising them enough. Imagine also that you don't happen to be the praising type—or, worse, that you don't think their work is particularly praiseworthy. You can grit your teeth and offer praise, but you'll feel inauthentic, and perhaps also resentful. And that, then, will undoubtedly impact the effectiveness of your message. So what do you do? One option is to customize your language. You might decide, for example, that you're not going to use superlatives like your colleagues do—such as "great job" or "fantastic work"—and instead will say something more evenhanded, like "The client was very pleased with your work." This isn't effusive, but it is positive and specific, and might get the job done in a way you can live with.

Jane Reddy—the military cadet—was someone else who ended up customizing her words in a very similar way. You might recall that Jane was deeply uncomfortable with the way her colleagues yelled, screamed, and berated younger cadets. She wanted to gain the cadets' respect as well—just not by humiliating them. Jane's solution was exactly in line with what we're talking about here: She customized her language and tone to get the message across, but in a way that felt far more humane. Instead of yelling, Jane decided to get around the confrontation simply by turning statements into questions, and to do so with a quiet intensity that challenged without humiliating the cadets. She'd pepper them with questions such as: "Did you have a strategy for why you shined your shoes but not your belt buckle? Were there competing priorities? Why did you pick the one you picked?" In the end, Jane customized a style that worked for her and that also achieved the respect she was looking for.

Another application of customization comes from Sangita Gupta, a customer service representative for an online company specializing in sourcing nannies and babysitters. Sangita's job was to respond via email to complaints the company received from disgruntled, confused, and frustrated customers. Because of the huge volume of emails the company received—along with the fact that many of these complaints were similar—the company had developed certain "scripted answers" for managing client complaints.

One recurring example was the company's automatic renewal system, whereby people would be automatically billed for services, often long after they used them. As it turned out, many customers were unaware of the billing system, which was explained in extremely fine print, and, as a result, ended up being charged extraordinary amounts of money for services they didn't use. From Sangita's perspective, this wasn't very fair. The customers had a point. But of course she couldn't exactly say that as a company rep; she had to represent the company. But in a way, to not feel terrible about doing her job, she also had to represent herself as well—so she really felt she was in a bind. The company was being sneaky—the disgruntled customers were correct—but she couldn't say anything.

So what did she do? The answer, actually, is just what we've been talking about: customization. Sangita found a way to customize her responses to clients in a way that didn't make her feel cold or robotic, or that she was toeing the company line.

For example, instead of providing the stock company

response "I'm sorry if you weren't aware of this policy," Sangita would write: "I sincerely apologize that this wasn't more clear" and "I'll be happy to share your feedback with my colleagues in the marketing group." It was a subtle change but an important one for Sangita, because she felt far more authentic delivering this message. She was truly sorry that the policy wasn't clear, and the company's version felt like it was placing too much blame on the customer, when, in fact, the policy wasn't that clear in the first place. While this didn't necessarily solve the problem, it made Sangita feel she was validating the customers' concerns and also, at the very least, offering a more personal connection.

Thus far, we've seen how people choose actual, scripted words as a way of customizing their role when stepping outside their comfort zones. Sometimes, however, the process of using language to customize our roles is a bit "looser": We don't literally script out what we have to say, but we try to steer conversations toward topics we're comfortable and familiar with—again, so we can play to our strengths in situations that might otherwise be quite challenging to perform in.

That was—and definitely still is—the case for Brenda

Dater, a good family friend and author of the book *Parenting Without Panic*, a book for parents of children with autism or Asperger's syndrome. Brenda's challenge (a challenge that I share) was the discomfort she felt playing the role of an "expert"—which is quite natural when you write a book, but quite unnatural if you appreciate all the complexity in the world and realize that few people are truly experts in anything. For Brenda, it was particularly uncomfortable playing the role of an expert in other parents' lives because she couldn't possibly understand the reality of their experiences the way they could. Yes, she could offer some general advice—and she did have confidence in the advice she was offering—but the "level" of expertise that people wanted her to display and communicate was way outside her comfort zone.

When Brenda spoke with PR agencies about promoting her book, they too told her she needed to embrace that "expert" role—to take a stand and be the voice for all parents out there. But Brenda didn't want to be the voice for all parents. How could she be—especially when much of that advice came in the form of a 140-character tweet? People's experiences with their children—and especially with their children who have disabilities—are deeply personal and specific. And the idea of dispensing sound-bite "wisdom" to the masses simply wasn't going to work. Frankly, if that's what it took to be a modern-day expert, it just wasn't going to fit Brenda.

This obviously created quite a conundrum: Brenda had written a book—and a good one at that—and she didn't want to crawl under a rock and hide. But at the same time, she didn't want to compromise who she was in the process. The answer to this bind, as it turned out, was precisely what we're talking about in this section of the book. Brenda used customization as a strategy for having her cake and eating it too: She shared her advice and wisdom and was able to be the type of leading authority on this important topic that she wanted to be— and that her publisher wanted her to be—but she did it on her own terms. After some trial and error, Brenda realized that stories—personal stories that she told about her own experience—were the number one best way for her to communicate with readers.

And Brenda had many stories to share. She too was a parent of a child with Asperger's (in fact, she had three kids, and another of her children had struggled with anxiety and ADHD as well), so when she shared her experiences and what's worked for her, it was coming from an authentic and vulnerable place. And as the director of child and teen services at a community-based autism and Asperger's organization, Brenda had many other stories to share as well. What was so critical to Brenda was the fact that she could share these insights and stories without feeling that she was compromising who she was.

Someone else who used customization to her advantage—though in a very different context—was Leslie Maker, a very successful Internet entrepreneur from New York City, who quite confidently told me when we met that she's terrible with numbers. "When I'm in a meeting pitching to VC's [venture capitalists]," Leslie said, "I'm terrible at understanding the nuances of LTV and CAC [lifetime value of a customer and customer acquisition cost]—which is all that many of these guys want to talk about. But what I'm really good at is ideas. I read tons of different stuff—I understand everything from art to physics to popular culture and am really good at putting it all together in creative ways." Leslie knows she needs to impress in these meetings, but instead of doing it through numbers, she does it through ideas: "I can draw parallels with my business that they've never heard of but that get them to think. I'll bring up something that happened on a hit TV show and then connect that to the fact that there's a new company in New York doing Uber for helicopters, and then I'll connect those two things to a key differentiator in what we're trying to do with our business. So, I impress, but not in the traditional way."

CUSTOMIZE YOUR BODY LANGUAGE

People also often customize by adjusting body language. Annie Jones used this tactic to her advantage when she confidently walked into Rick Schmitz's office unannounced and closed the door behind her, as if to say: "I mean business" without actually having to say it. Annie also used body language to psych herself up. Before even walking into Rick's office, Annie strutted up and down the hallways of her building, doing her best impression of the confident executive, to get her adrenaline pumping and her courage level up to its highest level possible. And when she burst into his office, she used more body language—standing up tall with her hands at her side or planting her hands firmly on Rick's desk.

When Annie told me this story, I was quite surprised and impressed at how quickly she had gone from utter fear to such a confident demeanor, but Annie told me that it really was mostly an act. She had desperately wanted to confront Rick—and she believed she had to confront him. But she had not felt anywhere near as confident as she appeared. In fact, part of the reason Annie planted her hands on Rick's desk in a "power pose" was that she was afraid she might actually faint! With her hands on the desk, she had much better balance.

What Annie might not have realized at the time was that, in addition to making herself appear more confident to Rick, changing her body language in this way may have made her *feel* more confident and powerful as well—likely making it easier, then, for her to portray these behaviors in an authentic and compelling way. It's like that famous lyric from the musical *The King and I* when the main character comforts her son about having to step outside their comfort zones to serve the King of Siam: "Whenever I feel afraid, I hold my head erect and whistle a happy tune so no one will suspect I'm afraid . . . The result of this deception is very strange to tell, for when I fool the people I fear, I fool myself as well."

In fact, several psychological studies conducted by Harvard professor Amy Cuddy, Berkeley professor Dana Carney, and INSEAD professor Andy Yap have shown that simply putting yourself into a "power pose" like Annie's can temporarily raise the level of "power hormones" (testosterone) in your body and reduce the level of "stress hormones" (cortisol)—thereby making you feel more powerful, more tolerant to risk-taking, and more effective in situations such as job interviews. And it wasn't just the pose that Annie used to peer over Rick at his desk. It's likely that the way she walked down those hallways, swinging her arms back and forth, had an effect as well, as these researchers have found that by simply sitting in tight, constricted positions—like in a too-small seat or hunched over a desk—we tend to feel more stressed and less powerful, compared to when we sit or stand in a more "expansive" pose like Annie's.

Power poses, however, aren't the only way people use body language to customize how they behave when stretching beyond their comfort zones. In some cases, body language can serve as a replacement for verbal behavior, especially when verbalizing a message in a particular situation might be particularly hard to do. The consultant you read about before, Wendy Lodge, did just this, in fact, when speaking up at meetings. She'd start by raising her hand, knowing that no one would actually "call on her" like in grade school but sensing that the hand raise would do something else important: it would signal that she had something to say. And then, she'd do it again—this time, actually leaning into the table while she did it, with one finger pointing into the air, again, pronouncing nonverbally that she has something to say! At this point, people would typically get the message and invite her to participate. So, it was a way of customizing behavior nonverbally to get the job done but in a way that worked for her. Incidentally, Wendy didn't use this tactic forever—in fact, over time she became increasingly comfortable simply interrupting, just like her colleagues did. But this creative use of nonverbal behavior, at least at first, was a tool for getting her over the hump.

CUSTOMIZE THE TIMING

Timing is another variable you can often manipulate to your advantage when trying to customize behavior that feels quite outside your comfort zone to perform. There are many different ways to manipulate time: You can choose a certain time of day over another to perform a task that's particularly challenging for you. You can use a certain time during the week. You can sequence a particular task after or before another task, and you can also do a particularly challenging aspect of a task at the beginning or end of a larger event. Wendy Lodge was able to use time to her advantage by employing a "pre-meeting" strategy. She shared her ideas with key decision makers beforehand, outside of the pressured environment of the actual meeting. Doing this enabled her to "stress test" her ideas, as she felt more comfortable hearing and responding to early critiques and challenges to her ideas in a one-on-one setting, Wendy could adjust and improve her ideas based on this early feedback. In fact, because of this strategy, Wendy started to feel increasingly confident walking into meetings because she had tested her ideas and now the decision makers knew she had something to contribute.

Wendy was able to use time to her advantage because she knew when she was going to be at her best—especially as a novice. Being knowledgeable about when you are going to be at your best in a particular situation is a great way of using time to customize acting outside your comfort zone, especially if the task you have to perform doesn't have any specific due date or deadline. For example, many managers I spoke with at the apparel company where we did our necessary evils research told me how they would schedule layoffs at times of the day when they personally felt most capable and lucid—for some, it was after having had the chance to do yoga or go on a long run. For others, it was doing the task sandwiched between activities they enjoy and that give them energy.

One manager, who knew he was going to be overwhelmed after having done the deed, purposely scheduled another "meeting" after doing a layoff; the meeting was really a meeting with himself—so he could take a long walk around the facility to regain his composure. And it's not just layoffs: I've also encountered many examples of people manipulating time as a strategic tool when it comes to stressful networking events. For example, one manager I spoke with who dreads networking events likes to purposefully go very early so he can start talking with people in a relatively small, intimate setting (before the throngs of people arrive). This then gets him more immersed in the setting, less stressed, and he feels like he can much more easily carry over this positive vibe into the main networking event itself. Another example of strategic use of time comes from author and thought leader Dorie Clark, an expert on networking and personal transformation, who often uses her own personal experience in her articles to inspire and educate others. This is what she wrote in a recent post about how she has proactively used time to her advantage:

> My circadian rhythms are fairly normal, but I'm definitely not a morning person. Early in my career, I dutifully signed up to attend five-hundred-person networking breakfasts, because "that's what you do" as a businessperson. I eventually realized the shock of waking up at 6 a.m. to get downtown

in time was making my entire day less productive,
so I swore them off. (I gave up early morning exer-
cise for the same reason.) For introverts, networking
requires a little more cognitive effort: It's fun, but
you have to psych yourself up to be "on." I don't
need to have the additional burden of doing it
when I'm tired. I now stack the deck in my favor by
refusing any meetings before 8 a.m. or after 9 p.m.

Another interesting case of using time to one's advantage comes from Drew Lyons, who, as you might recall
from earlier in the book, is an environmental consultant with an unfortunate phobia of networking events.
Drew didn't just feel uncomfortable at these events; he
resented the fact that he had to do them in the first place.
One trick, though, that seemed to work for him had to
do with this same topic of time. Drew hated schmooz-
ing, but he did really enjoy participating in anything of
substance—giving a speech at a conference, or, if he
wasn't selected for a talk, he'd always make sure to ask a
question or two during the Q & A so he could become
"known" at the event, not just as some schmuck who
would try to sell you on his services but as the guy who
made the thoughtful comment and probably has something legitimate to say. And the way he used time to his

advantage was to make this investment in the Q & A sessions early in the conference and then reap the dividends later, as people often remembered him and his comments and he could leverage this sense of expertise not only to gain people's respect but also, just as important, to feel more legitimate and comfortable about having these networking conversations in the first place.

Another way that many people in my research used time to their advantage was for preparation and pep talks. A number of professionals we spoke with in our necessary evils studies used preparation to facilitate performance: Doctors practiced in simulated emergency sessions, and sometimes on each other. Managers practiced with colleagues and with their HR managers. And officers rehearsed what they were going to do and say during evictions, both at the station and also in the car between evictions. In fact, many of the people I interviewed for this book, not surprisingly, reported that practicing was a way of easing their anxiety and perfecting their technique. Leslie Maker practiced her pitches to venture capitalists with other venture capitalists she knew. Lily Chang practiced what she was going to say to Julia with a close colleague who knew about the situation and helped coach Lily through the difficulties she faced.

And then, finally, people often reported psyching themselves up as a customization strategy. Many managers I spoke with described going to the bathroom to practice what they were going to say. They often described it as gearing up to play a role, or even to put on a mask. And speaking of pre-talk preparation, Leslie Maker told me she frequently would take a shot of whiskey before pitching to venture capitalists, just to take the edge off—a point echoed in how the *Atlantic*'s Scott Stossel described the elaborate cocktail of alcohol and drugs that he takes before an event simply to get through the situation:

> *Let's say you're sitting in an audience and I'm at the lectern. Here's what I've likely done to prepare. Four hours or so ago, I took my first half milligram of Xanax. (I've learned that if I wait too long to take it, my fight-or-flight response kicks so far into overdrive that medication is not enough to yank it back.) Then, about an hour ago, I took my second half-milligram of Xanax and perhaps 20 milligrams of Inderal. (I need the whole milligram of Xanax plus the Inderal, which is a blood-pressure medication, or beta-blocker, that dampens the response of the sympathetic nervous system, to keep my*

physiological responses to the anxious stimulus of standing in front of you—the sweating, trembling, nausea, burping, stomach cramps, and constriction in my throat and chest—from overwhelming me.) I likely washed those pills down with a shot of scotch or, more likely, vodka, the odor of which is less detectable on my breath. Even two Xanax and an Inderal are not enough to calm my racing thoughts and to keep my chest and throat from constricting to the point where I cannot speak; I need the alcohol to slow things down and to subdue the residual physiological eruptions that the drugs are inadequate to contain.

USE PROPS

Just like an actor does onstage, people can use props to customize behavior as well. That was certainly the case for Jennifer Cohen, a young rabbi I spoke with whose challenging situation was providing pastoral care to seniors more than twice her age. Jennifer was a private person by nature—and although she deeply cared about being helpful and present for the seniors she was working with, she also felt acutely uncomfortable about the idea of intruding on their privacy. But that wasn't the only challenge she experienced. She also really had no clue what to say when she entered the room. There would be a seventy-five- or eighty-year-old woman Jennifer had never met in her life, just sitting there in a room by herself, perhaps eating something or watching TV or sleeping, and Jennifer's role was to visit, be present, give her what she needed. But how could Jennifer tell what these people needed? And what could she possibly do or say to make this a meaningful interaction?

For months, Jennifer had no clue what to do. She'd tentatively enter rooms, feeling awkward and almost as if she were trespassing on a person's privacy more than paying them a visit. And even if they were fine to have her there, she simply didn't know what to say or do to fill that unscripted moment. Jennifer ended up finding a way out of the conundrum through customization. In her case, this meant using what she came to call her "bag of tricks." On the advice of a senior rabbi mentor, Jennifer decided to start bringing a bag of conversation starters, including books she was reading or thought the person she was visiting might enjoy, card games, and ritualistic items like candles, prayer books, and a kiddush cup. Sometimes she even brought freshly baked challah bread. In the end, the bag of tricks worked wonders. It eased the moment for Jennifer and also enabled her to make a personal connection with the people she was visiting—on terms they were comfortable with.

An additional, and somewhat unusual, example of using props to customize behavior comes from the banking executive we discussed earlier, Roger Evans, who experienced deep levels of frustration and resentment when he moved from a large financial firm where he essentially had control over his own projects, to a much smaller, consensus-driven firm where he had to work to get "buy-in" for everything he did. You might recall that Roger was initially quite frustrated that he had to make this switch in the first place, especially since he was so much more efficient doing projects on his own. Eventually, though, after developing a strong sense of conviction in the purpose of this transformation—which was to fit in, succeed at the new company, and also sharpen his collaboration skills—he was ready to give it a go . . . except for one thing: He wasn't sure how to do it.

Roger feared he'd either inadvertently revert to his default way of acting . . . or be misunderstood. Or both. So, to facilitate his foray into the world of collaboration, Roger created a unique, customized collaboration tool: a "guide to working with Roger Evans," which was an actual document that detailed in a very comprehensive way all of Roger's pet peeves, preferences, and areas he was working on improving at. The guide outlined "everything you'd need to know about Roger to work with him": from the font and formatting he preferred to a "key" for interpreting Roger's behavior. For example, one of the entries in the guide described how Roger might appear to show impatience when he's actually feeling excitement—and that if you're unclear, you should ask. While certainly unusual, the guide ended up serving a functional purpose for Roger—as a "scaffolding" tool to help him continue on his own journey toward becoming a more collaborative boss and colleague.

In my research, I came across many other cases of people using props to help them perform behavior outside their comfort zones. Pediatric physicians, for example, arranged to have bubble blowers available to distract children during painful procedures. Managers made tissue or candy available to people in rooms where they conducted layoffs. Managers also often scripted out the first few lines of a layoff so they could cover the "talking points" they had to hit, which enabled them to be spontaneous—and ideally authentic—throughout the rest of the conversation. Police officers would sometimes go against department protocol and offer milk, bottled water, and sandwiches to the people they were evicting as a gesture of respect, since people often lacked these very basic needs and were happy to receive the items.

An interesting celebrity example using props to help ease the challenges of acting outside your comfort zone comes from Larry David, cocreator of *Seinfeld* and the star and creator of the unscripted comedy series *Curb Your Enthusiasm*. In an effort to stretch himself artistically, David decided not only to write a scripted play but also to star in it, despite having not acted in a play since the eighth grade! And, as he revealed in a series of interviews in and around the play's opening on Broadway, the experience was terrifying. In an interview with late-night host David Letterman, David exclaimed: "I'm nervous. I'm frightened. I'm scared to death. Help me! Dave, help me! Help me!" And at another point during the run of the play, David's director, Anna Shapiro, found him backstage, sweaty, tearing off his sweater. In Shapiro's words: "He looked at me and he goes, 'How do people do this? How do they do this? This is crazy!"

Even though David had written the play, he had an extremely difficult time actually having to act in it—especially within the confines of a set script. David said: "It's completely different. I have total freedom on *Curb* to kind of say and do anything I want. I can follow every impulse that I have. I'm allowed to interject when other people are talking. I'm kind of writing the scene as we're doing it, but this play is a different animal. You have lines. There are cues that are very important. Yeah, you have to abide by the script, and the other actors don't like it if you get off of it, either." And then when asked if this was outside his comfort zone, David replied, "Yeah. If you even have a comfort zone . . . Whatever comfort zone I had was pretty narrow, but this was definitely out of it, for sure."

What ended up helping David cope with the great anxiety he felt performing his play onstage was just the kind of thing we've been talking about: He started wearing his own clothes onstage, especially after he felt so out of sorts wearing something that didn't feel authentic to him. "You know, everything I tried on I said, 'Why can't I just wear my own clothes?'" David explained to NPR reporter Melissa Block. "And they go, 'No, no, you can't. You don't wear your own clothes.' I go, 'Well, I'm wearing my own clothes.'" And in the end, perhaps aided in part by this subtle tweak that made him feel slightly more at home outside his comfort zone, David went on to at least partially enjoy the Broadway run despite his initial fear and trepidation—as his director noted: "As much as he was 'complaining' about it—I've never seen him look that alive, he had a sparkle in his eye. He was acting."

In my own efforts learning to stretch beyond my comfort zone while speaking in public, I've used plenty of props. The main prop I used for a very long time was a written set of notes that I'd bring with me onstage (typically, at that point in my career, at an academic conference or in an MBA classroom) that captured everything I wanted to say—verbatim—during the talk. I wouldn't literally read from these notes, but I'd rely heavily on them, like an actor doing a read-through with a new script, except in these cases I wasn't actually doing a practice read-through. These were real presentations, and my prop made me feel comfortable and—I realized in retrospect—helped me also stay well within my comfort zone.

Over time, however, as I started gaining confidence at presenting, seeing others present with no notes at all—and how audiences seemed to react positively to it—I decided I wanted to give note-less presentation a try. Now this was scary: I had never given a talk without notes. What if I didn't know what to say? What if I fainted? Could I pull it off? I eventually did pull it off, but to give myself a little added boost of confidence, I started wearing a special ring every time I presented.

That ring had a tiger-eye stone that my great-uncle happened to have found on a beach in the South Pacific during World War II. When he came back to the States after the war, he had it mounted into a simple silver ring, which I always admired whenever my family visited him. And that's why I was so excited when he eventually passed it on to me as a gift. I thought it was the coolest ring, and I also, I think, somehow made a connection between the ring and the war. It represented courage to me, and every time I gave a speech without notes, I slipped it onto my finger. I wore that ring for years—and never told anyone its meaning. People would ask about it, since it was a fairly striking and unusual stone. And I'd always tell the story of my great-uncle. But I never revealed its true meaning to me. Interestingly, as I have become much more accustomed to speaking without notes—and now to many different types of audiences—I no longer wear the ring.

And I am certainly not alone (or crazy) in using a lucky charm to help me get over the hump of a challenging task. In a recent study conducted by researchers in Germany and published in the prestigious journal *Psychological Science*, researchers found that people who were told they were playing with a "lucky" ball were far more successful at putting (which, as golfers know, is definitely the most nerve-racking part of the game) compared to those who weren't told their ball was lucky. Activating this superstition boosted people's confidence at the task and also improved their persistence when confronted with challenges—the same way that wearing the ring did for me during challenging public speeches. It's important to note, however, that you don't necessarily want to place all your eggs in one lucky ring basket. Ideally, the courage to act outside your comfort zone will become a part of you, something internal rather than external, placed not in the magic power of an object like a ring that could potentially get lost or misplaced but, instead, within your own developing powers. Despite this concern, I do have to say that it felt good to have that lucky ring on my hand in the early days. And as I mentioned before, I now no longer need or wear the ring.

CUSTOMIZE THE CONTEXT

In addition to using props, people can also stage the context itself to create the conditions for successful behavior flexing. For example, Richard Branson, chairman of Virgin Group, tries not to make traditional speeches but rather play to his strong suit, which is more honest, spontaneous communication. This is what he's had to say about his behavior flexing strategy: "Whenever possible I now try to arrange for less structured question-and-answer sessions rather than traditional twenty-five-minute speeches. It's not only less nerve-racking for me, but I also find that audiences get a lot more out of a session when they can jump in with questions rather than sitting there thinking, 'I wish he'd talk about XYZ.'"

The satirist Mark Twain—who was famously fearful of speaking in public—liked to strategically place people in the crowd who he knew would laugh at his jokes:

> *I had got a number of friends of mine, stalwart men, to sprinkle themselves through the audience armed with big clubs. Every time I said anything they could possibly guess I intended to be funny, they were to pound those clubs on the floor. Then there was a kind lady in a box up there, also a good friend of mine, the wife of the governor. She was to watch me intently, and whenever I glanced toward her she was going to deliver a gubernatorial laugh that would lead the whole audience into applause.*

Bringing people you know to a stressful event is a common way of customizing otherwise challenging situations. Internet entrepreneur Leslie Maker, for example, often brings an extroverted colleague with her to meetings with venture capitalists, especially when she thinks small talk will be in the cards, since small talk isn't Leslie's strong suit and she wants to use her preparation time to focus on the product and pitch instead of how to talk about the weather or commute to the office.

Staging is a key issue in medicine, especially for physicians who have to deliver bad news, such as a cancer diagnosis, to their patients. If you are a fan of the show *Mad Men*, you know that in the 1960s and 1970s most physicians actually considered it inhumane to disclose bleak cancer diagnoses to patients. But that has, of course, changed in recent years and physicians have gone to great lengths to develop best practices around the delivery of bad news, including building important protocols for staging the context. Doctors are trained to arrange for privacy—by finding a private room, ideally, but if that's not available, by drawing the curtains around a patient's bed and having tissues available in case the patient is upset. Doctors are also encouraged to give patients the choice of including significant others in the discussion, and they are also urged to sit rather than stand, not only as a signal that they're not there to rush through the conversation but also because sitting down typically relaxes the patient. Physicians are also instructed to inform the patient ahead of time about any time constraints they might expect, or interruptions that could interfere with the conversation.

Another technique to arranging the context to fit your needs is to strategically sit or stand in a particular location that suits you as a way of customizing your behavior. Imagine, for example, that you were a new student in a classroom at Harvard Business School and by nature you weren't the participating type. However, to succeed in your classes and get the recognition of your professor and your classmates you had to somehow conquer your fear. As it turns out, that was exactly the situation Jenna (a colleague of mine) faced: She used a customization technique along the lines of what we're discussing here.

Jenna didn't have a lot of work experience—certainly not compared to her Harvard Business School colleagues. She also was shy, unassuming, and quite modest. And, as you might expect, she had a very difficult time participating in class. The problem, of course, is that at Harvard, as at many other universities, classroom participation counts a lot for your final grade. And not only that—it's embarrassing to say nothing in class, especially when you're trying to impress your fellow classmates—and future networking buddies—in addition to your professor.

But Jenna felt completely stymied—and terrified of

the only two options she had: saying anything or saying nothing. But she did want to succeed, and realized that as someone coming from a research background, she might have insights different from the norm. So, she went for it—but not without customizing the context, which, in her case, meant sitting right in the front of the classroom—in the very first row—for two reasons. First, on that odd occasion she did get the courage to speak, it would be pretty easy for the professor to notice her. But even more important, by sitting in the front she wouldn't have to actually see any of the other eighty people in the room. It would feel just like her and the professor, although, of course, behind her there would be eighty people with outstretched hands aching to get their two cents into the conversation.

So, in various ways, staging a setting can be a helpful tool for behavior flexing. It puts the power back in your hands, enabling you to find ways of taking a situation outside your comfort zone and putting it right back inside your comfort zone, one tweak at a time.

CHAPTER 5

Clarity: The Power of Honest Perspective

When Linda Rogers started Easy Family Travel from her house, she never thought that in-person networking would be such an important part of her business. For years, Linda had worked as an in-house corporate travel agent, but with two children under five and a husband working a job with equally long hours, something had to give. At first, the new gig felt perfect. She'd joke with her husband in the morning that she was "off to work!"—which meant walking from the kitchen to the living room table: the shortest commute in history. But as the reality of running a small business set in, Linda realized she was going to have to start doing something she had always dreaded doing: sales pitches about her business. And that's where things got difficult.

By nature, Linda was an introvert—and she was also modest and private. She didn't like to toot her own horn or pitch or promote herself, and was deeply uncomfortable speaking in public. So, when opportunities came up to pitch the business, Linda did what we all would now recognize as Avoidance 101: She told herself she was too busy—or that she really needed to work on the website or social media instead. Or, in a few cases, she sent her college intern to events instead of representing the company herself. Linda had convinced herself that these networking and sales opportunities weren't all that important for the business and that she was doing the right thing by avoiding them. But in the end, of course, they were important. The business took a very long time to get off the ground, and a great deal of that difficulty was a direct result of Linda's inability to look herself in the mirror and see how she was avoiding something she really needed to engage with. Without this sense of clarity and self-awareness—that she was scared and anxious and desperately doing anything she could to avoid acting outside her comfort zone—the chances of her ever actually taking the leap were very small, if not impossible.

Clarity as an Antidote to Avoidance

What Linda really needed here is what we all need as a precursor to doing anything outside our comfort zones—and that's clarity: about the fact we're avoiding . . . about the *ways* we're avoiding . . . and about how we're *rationalizing* to ourselves that avoidance isn't really avoidance, and is perfectly functional and acceptable. Think of clarity as an antidote to the defenses that we put up to protect us from tasks outside our comfort zones. It's honest, self-reflective psychological accounting: an attempt to be as true as possible with ourselves about the situations we're currently working on, taking a careful inventory of our true feelings—even if we're embarrassed by them—as well as an inventory of our avoidance strategies.

For example: When you avoided speaking to your boss all last week, was that truly a random occurrence, as you told yourself, or might it have been because you were terrified he might ask you to take on that new leadership role? Or, when you declined yet another opportunity to speak in public, was it really because you were too busy or you didn't think these opportunities were so important for your career . . . or was it perhaps because you're afraid of stepping onstage? Looking at yourself in the mirror and admitting flaws is hard for most people. But it's an essential precursor for acting outside your comfort zone. As Dale Wimbrow wrote in the classic poem "The Guy in the Glass": "When you get what you want in your struggle for life, and the world makes you King for a day, then go to the mirror and look at yourself, and see what that guy has to say . . . You may fool the whole world down the pathway of life, and get pats on your back as you pass. But your final reward will be heartaches and tears if you've cheated the man in the glass."

Clarity as a Normalizer to Distorted Thinking

Clarity serves another key function as well: It counteracts our tendency to engage in what psychologists call "distorted" or "exaggerated" thinking. Imagine, for example, walking into your boss's office for what you assume is a regular meeting, but instead finding out that you're being considered for a major new position in your company. You're shocked, but also worried. And as you "sleep on it" at home, stressful thoughts flood your brain: *How could they possibly think I could do this job? I'm such a terrible fit. I can't see any way I could succeed at this.* In distorted or exaggerated thinking, we take the legitimate fears we have and pump them up to a level that feels practically intolerable.

In other words, instead of a job being merely difficult or challenging, it's impossible. Or instead of experiencing a bumpy road at the beginning, the entire situation will likely be an "utter failure." Especially with little experience and confidence in a particular situation, we can exaggerate the challenges associated with acting outside our comfort zones and think something is outside our comfort zones—in fact, way outside our comfort zones— when it actually isn't.

But even those of us with a great deal of experience can suffer from distorted thinking. You'd be surprised at how pervasive this distorted thinking is, even among people who, by any conventional standard, should have a fairly clear picture of their own abilities and expertise. Here, for example, is what Michelle Pfeiffer said about herself: "I still think people will find out that I'm really not very talented. I'm really not very good. It's all been a big sham." And this comes from poet Maya Angelou: "I have written eleven books, but each time I think, 'Uh-oh, they're going to find out now. I've run a game on every-body, and they're going to find me out.'" And I personally experience these feelings all the time, for example, when speaking to audiences in an academic or corporate set-ting, or sitting on a panel. I often wonder what I could possibly have to say that's insightful and interesting and novel enough to merit being invited to a particular dis-cussion or panel.

And that's where clarity comes in. Clarity is the abil-ity to "normalize" your reactions and perceptions of a situation so that distorted thinking doesn't sabotage your behavior—which might mean avoiding or declining the opportunity because of your distorted predictions. Incidentally, exaggerated thinking doesn't have to be only negative. You can have equally intense and unreal-istic thoughts on the positive side of the spectrum as well, thinking to yourself that upon taking the job you'll be crowned a leadership prodigy, for example—an hon-orable goal, no doubt, but one that, we'd likely all agree, is quite unrealistic for the situation.

Clarity Sounds Great, but How Do You Make It Happen?

We all would probably like to have this type of even-handed, clear thinking, but the question is, how do we achieve it? Luckily, there are plenty of routes toward gaining clarity, and most of them start at the notion of stepping away, or stepping aside, to get a different perspective and a more "detached" vantage point on what we're potentially struggling with.

A few years ago at a research group I was part of at Harvard University, we had a very interesting discussion about the places where we tend to get inspiration for our work—where we get the very best ideas. What was so interesting to me about this discussion is that every single one of the suggestions (at least the ones I remember well) had to do with stepping away to gain clarity and perspective. Some people, for example, said they got their best ideas during a massage—lying there half-conscious as their minds fluttered from thought to thought and the therapist's hands wrung the worry and fear away from their minds. Others felt their best ideas came while walking, or biking, or running, or even showering! My best ideas, by the way, typically come while walking my dog. Since this realization of where my best ideas come from, I've been fascinated with this idea of stepping away to gain clarity—and in researching the topic, I've discovered that it isn't just our research group at Harvard who uses the tactic.

STEP AWAY

For example, in his book *Daily Rituals*, author Mason Currey details how Beethoven would always go for a long walk after lunch, carrying a pencil and paper in hand to record his inspirations. The composer Gustav Mahler would follow a similar routine, as would Benjamin Britten, using psychological separation and distance as a tool for fueling creative thought. And it's not just walking. Microsoft chairman Bill Gates would use personal isolation as a tool for achieving clarity about his business. Twice a year, Gates underwent what he called a "Think Week" ritual: total isolation for seven days, reading papers, pondering ideas, and considering the future of technology and Microsoft.

Many of the people you've read about in this book have used this strategy as well. You might also remember the story of Jane Reddy (the military cadet from earlier in the book), who used this same strategy of stepping aside to gain perspective on the traumatic episode with the younger cadet, and how critical it was for her to develop an authentic leadership style: something that was effective in the setting but that felt genuine and humane. And it was only by being away from the situation that she was able to truly reflect on what had happened and, most important, what kind of leader she really wanted to be. Lily Chang used this strategy as well. If you recall, Lily was the Internet entrepreneur who had to fire her best friend, Julia, because her ineptitude was threatening the livelihood of the small company. When Lily was face-to-face with Julia, it was difficult to think about anything other than their friendship, the hard times Julia had been experiencing at home, and how devastating it would be for her to receive this news. And, frankly, it was only by stepping away that Lily could see a clearer picture of the entire situation: Julia's troubles were having a cascading effect on the rest of the company, and multiple livelihoods were in play—Julia's for sure, but also Lily's, her employees', and her investors'. And once she was able to step away to see the entire picture, Lily was able to embrace the fact that Julia had to go and that Lily had to be the one to deliver the negative message.

REFER TO YOURSELF IN THE THIRD PERSON

As it turns out, Lily could have boosted her clarity even in the moment by using yet another strategy: telling herself that she could pull it off, especially if she did so by referring to herself in the third person (as in, "Lily, you can do this") as opposed to using the pronoun "I" (as in, "I can do this"). It sounds miraculous, and Ethan Kross, a psychology professor from the University of Michigan, also thought so when he first started doing studies about this technique, but across a series of studies, Kross has found striking evidence for this effect: When we engage in "self-talk," especially in stressful and difficult situations, we gain confidence and clarity simply from the slight psychological detachment of referring to ourselves in the third person.

For example, in one of his studies, Kross asked eighty-nine men and women to prepare a speech about why they were qualified for their "dream job." Half of the participants were instructed to use only first-person pronouns (e.g., "I") to describe themselves in a document they completed before the study, whereas the other half were simply asked to use their first names (e.g., "Andy"). Those who used their first names ended up approaching the task with less anxiety and more confidence. Additionally, after giving the speech, those who used their name instead of the pronoun ended up performing better and engaged in less rumination and worry after the fact. By simply referring to themselves in the third person, and perhaps also thinking about themselves in the third person (like, "Andy, you can do it" instead of "I can do it"), people were able to gain just that little bit of psychological distance they needed to even out their reactions.

And interestingly, these slight changes in perspective and language are reflected in patterns in our brains. In follow-up work, Kross put student volunteers into a brain-scanning machine and found that when these people talked about themselves in this detached, third-person perspective, their brain scans were more similar to those of other students who were simply giving advice to friends compared to those who used the first-person pronouns identified above.

This study is an example of a larger body of research in psychology that has shown powerful effects of "self-distancing" on the anxiety we experience in stressful situations. When we step back mentally and see our perceptions as only one way of seeing a particular situation, or when we imagine different ways of seeing the same situation (such as from another person's point of view), we have a clearer and more evenhanded perspective on a situation, which leads to less anxiety over time. We can do this by referring to ourselves in the third person, as the studies above illustrated. We can also achieve a similar effect by imagining how others might describe the situation we're in, or whether we think people who we know and trust, and who know and trust us, would see the distorted thoughts that we have in a particular situation as reasonable or realistic. If we do this thought exercise, and think to ourselves, "no they wouldn't," or even if we start to feel an inkling of doubt, that experience alone can help us start down the path toward clarity in our thinking.

PRACTICING SELF-REFLECTION

Fascinating research from James Pennebaker and his lab at the University of Texas at Austin has shown that simply writing about stressful events after the fact—even for a short time and over the course of a few days—can have a tremendous impact on our level of clarity, sharpening our thinking, reducing distress, and even leading to a strengthened immune system. For example, in one study Pennebaker and his colleagues asked HIV/AIDS patients to write either about their negative life experiences or their daily schedule. As predicted, the patients who ended up writing about life experiences measured higher on lymphocyte counts, which is a key marker for immune functioning. Again, as was the case with Kross's pronouns, writing about your experiences is a subtle yet powerful way to gain clarity in an emotionally charged situation—which, as we've seen, can have additional powerful effects on your effectiveness and well-being.

In work and in life, we all have a wide range of positive and negative experiences, but when we're caught in the throes of distorted or exaggerated thinking, it's often the negatives or the failures that loom large—especially when we compare our own personal behind-the-scenes struggles to others' "highlight reels." To counteract this tendency and do his part to increase the transparency of failure and the importance of balancing both positives and negatives, University of California, San Diego, neuroscience professor Bradley Voytek did something very interesting. He created a section toward the end of his CV titled "Rejections and Failures." I personally have seen hundreds of academic CVs—and have never seen anything like this, but it's fascinating. In this section, Voytek details his failures in great detail—including the fact that he was "ejected" from his undergraduate institution for a low GPA, how he had countless rejected journal papers and grants, and how when applying for jobs, he received only one acceptance. We so often judge our own accomplishments in life in relation to our perceptions of others, and it's so refreshing to see this example of balance and clarity in action.

FINDING CLARITY THROUGH SOMEONE ELSE'S EYES

Finally, one last, but truly essential resource for gaining clarity in a stressful situation is an insightful coach or mentor. If you think about it, very few of us in life go at it alone—especially in the types of "stretch" situations we're talking about in this book. And so we often enlist the help of a coach or a mentor to bring psychological clarity to our lives by reducing the distorted and exaggerated thinking that clouds our judgment and interferes with our behavior. That was certainly the case for Roger Evans, the banking executive we met earlier, who felt resentful when switching from a large financial firm, where he essentially had control over his own projects, to a much smaller, consensus-driven firm, where he had to work to get "buy-in" for everything he did. If you recall, Roger was frustrated he had to make this switch in the first place, especially since he felt fully capable of doing everything on his own. But with the help of a coach, he was able to see the effect his behavior—even his subtle nonverbal behavior—was having on other people. The coach would videotape meetings where Roger was present and then in separate sessions show Roger the videotape and demonstrate quite literally the effect that his behavior was having on others. Roger's coach also encouraged him to complete 360-degree performance evaluations, where Roger would receive detailed evaluations of his work style from subordinates, superiors, and peers. These tools gave Roger a completely different set of data about his actions and the effect they were having on others—and, in Roger's mind, were the key catalyst for his willingness to finally take steps to change his behavior.

Someone who provided me with a tremendous sense of clarity was my graduate school advisor, Richard Hackman. At the time, I was writing my first book, *Global Dexterity*, and it was something I felt deeply insecure about for multiple reasons. First of all, in the academic world—or at least in my corner of the academic world—books aren't typically valued—that is, not valued as much as articles. And so I was unsure if writing a book could be a "career killer." To top it off, I was also quite anxious and insecure about whether I could actually pull off a project like this. I started down my own path of distorted, negative thinking: "What if the book is a total flop?" "What if everyone in academics laughs at me for dedicating all my time to *this*?" "And what if I can't pull it off?"

And that's where Richard came in. At the time, I had been out of graduate school for quite a while, so Richard didn't really have any obligation to help me. But that didn't seem to matter. Richard's advice was simple. "Do it," he'd said. "Okay," I'd responded, wanting to make sure he truly understood my ambivalence about everything. "You have to do this," he continued. "You don't just want to speak to academics. You want to speak to people who actually struggle with this stuff. And it's going to be a great book."

Richard's advice cut right through the ambivalence I had been struggling with. Richard had always been— and still is, several years after his death—exactly the type of academic I always wanted to be: respected by other academics but with a deep interest in practice and in making a difference in the world. As a follow-up, Richard sent me an email a few days later that I still cherish. Here's what he said: "Hi, Andy. The book draft is really great . . . you have an extraordinary ability to write engaging examples and then draw from them the lessons to be learned. This will be extremely valuable to lots and lots of people both in this country and abroad. . . . You've really learned a lot, and accomplished a lot, in this line of work—and it shows! My heartiest congratulations."

YOUR OWN RECIPE

Remember that picture I talked about earlier? The one with the comfort zone circle and then the other circle, off in the distance, representing the "magic" that happens when you can somehow stretch outside your comfort zone and take a chance? What we just discussed—the three critical resources of behavior flexing—is what you need to create that critical bridge from one circle to the other: to move from a place of fear to a place of discovery and challenge . . . to move from a place you're comfortable—but limited—to a place where you can truly learn and grow.

If you like to cook (as I do), you've probably come across the distinction between a precise recipe and a flexible recipe. A precise recipe for a salad, for example, might dictate the exact type of lettuce to use; the precise measures of cucumber, carrots, peppers, and fixings you should include; and then the specific ingredients you need to make the salad dressing. A flexible recipe, on the other hand, is also used to make a salad, but on your own terms. This recipe might suggest a range of potential lettuces and toppings you could consider, along with a variety of oils and vinegars to experiment with to develop your own personal creation. As you can probably tell, what you've just read about self-awareness, conviction, and customization is this latter, more flexible type of framework. Self-awareness, conviction, and customization are the categories, but you need to fill in for yourself what makes sense for your particular case. You might find that certain ways of customizing your behavior are what enable you to really thrive and overcome the emotions that would otherwise have made you want to avoid your situation altogether. And the same goes with conviction: The way I justify and rationalize and make sense of why it is truly worthwhile, legitimate, and important for me to act outside my comfort zone in my situation will likely be totally different from how you make sense of your situation. Just as I might like mushrooms in a salad and you might prefer artichokes, each of us will personalize our own recipe for behavior flexing as necessary. I've offered up the categories of ingredients and now it's on you to experiment and create your own recipe for taking the leap.

CHAPTER 6

The Surprising Benefits of Taking a Leap

A manda, you can do this," Amanda Nickerson said to herself, wiping the sweat off her brow as she entered the building for her first interview in a very long time. She had met this contact on LinkedIn, which she had joined only a week before. It was all happening so quickly—maybe too quickly, but Amanda knew it was time. Her kids could take care of themselves. In fact, her oldest was applying to colleges! If he could take that step in his life, this was something Amanda could do as well.

Amanda never thought she'd be out of the job force for ten years, but, in her words, it "basically just kind of happened." All along, the plan had been to go right into the workforce following her PhD in economics, which, in her case, meant going into a tenure-track job in academics, teaching courses, advising students, and publishing papers. But, as often happens, life intervened. Amanda had her first child, Liam, in graduate school, and then soon after grad school, she had Lilly. There was no way at that time she was going to go the full professional route, especially with two children under two. Amanda wanted to be with the kids. Her husband supported the decision. And that was that: Only a few years removed from getting a PhD Amanda was a mom—full-time—and the idea of a full-time teaching and research career had become a pretty distant memory.

And for a while at least, it felt right. The kids were young and they needed her. But as time marched on and the kids got older and more independent, Amanda felt less and less necessary. And when her oldest started applying to colleges and working on his résumé, Amanda decided, "This is ridiculous," thinking, *My kid has a résumé and I don't? This just doesn't seem right.*

But the problem was that Amanda had been out of the game for so long that even the thought of putting herself out there was terrifying. For starters, Amanda was embarrassed about her résumé. The education section looked pretty good, but there was this massive gap in her work experience, and she wasn't sure she could actually put down "full-time mom" on her list of accomplishments, despite the fact that the job was pretty demanding, and, as her husband always said, much harder than anything he ever had to do at work.

And then there was the networking, and small talk, and self-promotion. Amanda was an introvert: She didn't love chatting up strangers, and certainly didn't like trying to convince them of all her wonderful capabilities. And even beyond that, she also was someone who absolutely hated imposing on other people. In fact, that more than anything else was what kept her up at night and stopped her from pushing "send" on emails she had carefully composed to potential contacts. She hated feeling like she was begging people for their time. And this felt especially uncomfortable because she didn't feel so comfortable about what she was "selling" in the first place. What could she contribute? What did she have to add?

But despite all the discomfort, Amanda was determined to give it a go. She didn't want to live her life regretting never having gone back to work, when part of her clearly wanted to try. And, frankly, her family could also use the income. That piece actually became very clear to her when, one day, she received a call from someone at her husband's workplace saying he had collapsed on the floor and was being rushed to the hospital. Thoughts flooded Amanda's mind—about her husband, the family, their well-being—and also whether the family could actually survive financially, if, God forbid, something awful actually did happen. In the end, he was okay (it was just dehydration), but that experience was the tipping point for her: She had to get back to work. It was time.

As predicted, the first few professional conversations were awkward—actually quite awkward—but once she got into the swing of things and was feeling a bit more comfortable, Amanda made what was, for her, a startling discovery: People were far more generous than she could ever have predicted. Prior to taking the leap, Amanda had this awful image in her mind of what it would be like for her—a "relative nothing"—to walk into a busy important person's office asking for help. But the reality, as she discovered from actually taking the leap and going for it, was 100 percent different from her expectations: People were nice; they were generous; they were encouraging; and they didn't seem to mind talking with her at all. And to Amanda's complete surprise, she also started to enjoy the process. She liked meeting people, making connections, and, eventually, even talking about job possibilities. And for Amanda, this was the biggest aha of the entire episode. What she had feared all along had become something she enjoyed.

The Incredibly Powerful Effect of Simply Giving It a Try

One of the most surprising aspects of my research has been the extent to which people so often seem to find interesting discoveries about things that they initially feared. It's a bit like trying a completely new food you've always been a bit afraid of. You may not like it; in which case, your initial fear would be justified. But what if you did like it? In fact, what if that food was one of the most wonderful things you've ever tasted—and you can't quite believe you never gave it a try?

Granted, this doesn't always happen: There are certainly situations that are so deeply stressful and difficult that simply giving it a go doesn't make the behavior feel any more palatable. But in so many cases I've witnessed—and experienced for myself—there is a very powerful

149

effect of giving something a try. And the "engine" for this effect, what makes taking that leap so powerful, is what I like to call personal discovery: what you learn about yourself, about the situation you've been struggling with, and, most important, about yourself *in* that situation you've been struggling with.

When you avoid a challenging situation out of fear or worry or potential embarrassment, you never get to benefit from the power of discovery. But when you do muster up the courage to give it a shot, you may be quite surprised at what you discover on the other side. That certainly was the case for Ella Cheng, a sophomore at Princeton running for class senator but terrified of what she had to do to win the seat. Ella had initially become interested in student government in high school, running for and, eventually, winning class president. But that was high school, where a few posters on the wall and free candy in the hallway could pretty much win the day. At her university, which was hundreds of times larger than her high school, things would be completely different. She'd have to go door to door to meet with her potential constituents, convincing them that they should vote for her—and not for the other people running for the seat. It was serious business—and the most challenging aspect of all was the self-promotion she feared she'd have to do to secure people's votes. As a lifelong introvert and a pretty modest person to boot, Ella dreaded these impromptu, unscripted conversations with strangers—then add in the fact that she had to pitch and promote herself like a product, and it became practically intolerable. But there was something about this opportunity to serve that appealed to her.

Ella had loved being class president in high school and was really able to make a difference. She had been inspired by the stories she heard from public servants—judges, politicians, and philanthropists—who came to speak at her high school to tell their stories. There was no other position where she could make that size of a difference for so many people. And so running for class office in college was the logical next step. So Ella went for it—and the big surprise for her was that she truly liked it! Granted, it was exhausting. During one election, she spoke with three hundred people in just three weeks. But many of these conversations ended up being deeply valuable and validated the reasons that Ella wanted to get into public service in the first place.

Interestingly, the most meaningful conversations weren't the ones where she promoted herself or asked people to vote for her. The magic really happened when she shifted her stance to ask people about their lives and what would make them better. She was able to learn about the struggles students had—with financial aid, relationships, burnout, housing—a gamut of issues with which Ella herself identified and where she felt she could really make a difference. Ella eventually won her election for student office and just a year later was named president of the entire undergraduate student body.

At some point you too will take the leap. And what I want to tell you is that you probably will be very surprised at what's on the other side of the threshold. Imagine, for example, that you are absolutely terrified of putting yourself out there and promoting yourself at a networking event. You dread making small talk (although you never really try doing it that much), and you feel awkward, unnatural, and overly self-promotional tooting your own horn. Imagine, though, that at some point, you realize that you have to give it a try; it's critical for your career and you're frankly a bit tired of hiding in the shadows as your colleagues and classmates put themselves out there and find interesting opportunities for themselves. So, you decide to give it a go. You start at smaller events, accompanied by a close friend, since that makes you a bit more comfortable, and you even practice what you might say to potential contacts with that friend. And as you walk up to the building and hear the buzzing conversation inside and catch a glimpse of people talking and laughing and exchanging business cards, you clench your teeth, push aside your anxiety, and just walk right into that room.

I'm hoping that this type of situation—or a version of this situation—resonates with you. And remember, it doesn't have to be a networking event. You can substitute any situation you want here—asking your boss for a raise, speaking up at a meeting, making a sale, delivering bad news. My point is that when you take that leap, you can start to experience a previously terrifying situation through an entirely new set of eyes.

The Amazing Power of Simply Taking a Leap

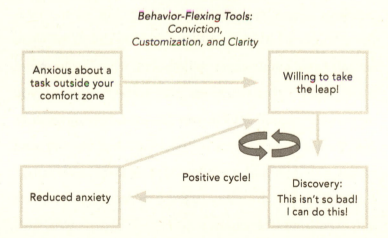

Behavior-Flexing Tools:
Conviction,
Customization, and Clarity

Anxious about a task outside your comfort zone → Willing to take the leap!

Reduced anxiety ← Positive cycle! ← Discovery: This isn't so bad! I can do this!

Remember the picture of the dysfunctional negative cycle that comes from avoiding tasks outside your comfort zone? I now want to show you another picture, one that captures the *positive* cycle that comes from using customization, clarity, and conviction to give yourself enough courage to take the leap.

As you can see, the diagram on page 153 starts at the same point that the previous one did: with you feeling anxious about a task outside your comfort zone. But here, instead of avoiding the task and perpetuating the "dysfunctional" cycle of avoidance, you use the tools you've learned here—conviction, customization, and clarity—to give yourself the courage and wherewithal to take that leap. And that's where the "magic happens." When you take that leap, you are able to benefit from personal discovery. Instead of imagining what something might be like—and likely fearing the worst—you actually now know what it *is* like. And what I've found in many cases is that when you give something a try, you might be surprised at what you discover. You may realize that the task you were dreading for so long isn't as hard as you thought, and, perhaps, isn't as awful as you had imagined either. In many cases, you might find aspects you even somewhat enjoy.

And when you feel that this isn't so bad and that you

can actually do it, your anxiety diminishes, you're likely willing to take the leap again the next time around, and all of a sudden you're in a positive loop: a cycle of learning and growth and experimentation and development that's very different from the cycle of fear and avoidance we talked about earlier in the book!

I can't tell you how many people have told me how shocked they are that after finally trying something new, they discover how fun it is . . . or how surprisingly unstressful it feels . . . or how exciting it can be . . . and, most important, how they never would have discovered this if they hadn't had the courage and conviction to make it happen in the first place. So with this in mind let's look at two core epiphanies people often have when taking the leap: (1) *This isn't so bad after all*, and (2) *I'm better at it than I thought*.

DISCOVERY #1: THIS ISN'T SO BAD AFTER ALL!

It wasn't every day that Jesus walked into the coffee shop and ordered a latte. But then again, this wasn't a regular day. It was December 24—Christmas Eve—and barista Jack Wagner had just started his shift, working the register and pouring lattes, just like he usually did. Jack had been working at the shop for about a year, as a mid-career transition. As a fiftysomething in a world of bearded and barefoot millennials, Jack was definitely an anomaly. But after burning out as an accountant in the corporate world, Jack knew he had to try something different. And this was definitely different—mostly because he had to constantly interact with people, especially clients, who entered the café wanting not only coffee but also an "experience." And it was Jack's job to provide that. But unfortunately, as an introvert who didn't really get the point of making small talk, Jack struggled to engage with customers.

With a combination of jealousy and awe, Jack watched how his colleagues would so easily chat up customers, making small talk about the weather or the coffee or pretty much anything. The jealousy part was that Jack wished he could do that too—or at least, he knew he needed to develop that skill to succeed at the job and also carry it into other aspects of his life. The awe part was that he couldn't quite believe how effortlessly people could have these casual conversations.

At his core, Jack thought small talk was useless—and inefficient. If you're here for a coffee, why not just have that simple transaction without all the bells and whistles of a meaningless awkward conversation? But Jack knew others didn't feel that way—and, most important, that the culture at the café was a small talk culture: The company wanted its people to engage and connect with customers. Aside from this challenge, Jack loved all other aspects of the work—the flexible hours, the pay, the unlimited caffeine . . . so he bit the bullet and decided he was going to give it a shot and take that leap. But it wasn't easy.

Customers would come up to the counter and Jack would panic, wondering whether he should say anything and if so, what exactly he should say. He'd obsess in his head so much that he'd forget drink orders—which then, of course, made any hope for a positive interaction that much more precarious. And with avoidance of small talk came more avoidance. Jack knew he had to say something—anything—to get the ball rolling. But he couldn't make the leap. That is, until Jesus walked in the door.

The resemblance was uncanny: the long, flowing hair; the beard; the white robe; and even sandals (in the middle of winter). He walked up to the cash register and ordered a cappuccino. And just then, Jack realized he had the perfect thing to say. This was going to be it—his moment. And as the man ordered his drink, Jack rehearsed the line in his head: *"Are you sure you want a cappuccino? Don't you want to just take a cup of water and turn it into a cappuccino yourself?"* But as the transaction unfolded, Jack said nothing. He couldn't pull the trigger. And as Jesus sauntered to the door and out the café, Jack felt awful about himself—again. If Jesus couldn't coax it out of him, Jack was definitely a lost cause!

That was until, unbelievably, someone else even more recognizable walked into the room. This man was burly but jovial and had a big fluffy white beard and glasses (and by the way, I'm not making this up). "Can I have a name?" Jack asked, thinking to himself, *This time I have to say something.* "Nicholas," said the man, with a straight face. And then it just came out: "You've got to be kidding," Jack exclaimed. "Are you serious?!" "Yeah," said the man. "I get it all the time. Here—look." The man rolled up his sleeve to expose a huge tattoo of the name "Nicholas" right there on his arm. Jack laughed again, and effortlessly—for the first time ever—just started chatting and making small talk. And it didn't stop with Saint Nick. Jack kept making small talk with other customers—and to his great surprise, started to like it. Previously, he thought small talk was irrelevant, but now he realized that it was quite nice—a chance to make a personal connection with someone, and sometimes to learn something you never knew. It just felt good to Jack to have these interactions and, over time, totally "made" the job.

One of the most profound transformations that I personally witnessed, where taking a leap led to an amazing discovery, took place in a semester-long course I taught at Brandeis. As part of the course, I required students to choose a situation outside their comfort zones and to work on improving their courage and confidence in the situation using many of the same tools I'm introducing to you in this book. The example I wanted to share with you was that of a shy Vietnamese MBA student who we'll call Thao. Thao chose the challenging situation of learning to participate in classroom debates and discussions. If you come from the United States, you might not find this situation unique or particularly challenging (although I, for one, did as a student and I know many other American-born students who do as well). But for Thao—who came from a culture without classroom participation or outward conflict in class—participating in these vigorous classroom debates felt incredibly uncomfortable and far outside her personal comfort zone.

Here is how Thao described the challenge early in the semester as part of the diary she kept for the class project:

Vietnamese culture highly values social harmony and thus doesn't allow actions that can break it. Arguing with other people in public, telling them you are right (and thus they are wrong), causes them to lose face. And causing people to lose face in public is a taboo in most Asian countries, especially in Vietnam. That's why I felt so bad speaking out in class and/or proving that I was right. I knew back then participating in the U.S is required to get good grades but somehow deep inside I felt like I was doing something very wrong. I was trembling, sweating. I just couldn't look at the professor in the eyes. I felt guilty.

One of the nice things about this project is that, in a sense, I can make sure people take that leap we've been talking about by requiring them to do the behavior. Of course, I don't grade people on how "well" they do it, just on how eloquently and thoughtfully they write about their experience, good or bad. I also make sure that conviction is part of the picture as well, because I ask them to choose a situation that is something they truly want to improve at. And that's why Thao chose classroom participation. She was an excellent student—a Fulbright scholar, in fact—and had very high standards for herself in terms of grades. And as it happened, classroom participation at the university counted a great deal toward course grades—sometimes as much as 50 percent of the final grade. So, the motivation was there and Thao desperately wanted to succeed.

The reason I tell this story is because of what happened to Thao during the semester. Almost all students made personal progress during their class projects—taking a situation they feared and making it into something they had a much greater understanding of and a far greater sense of the challenges they faced. Several students also made significant progress in overcoming the challenges of acting outside their comfort zones, even starting to like doing the behavior they initially feared. Thao was an extreme example of this pattern because after only a relatively short time—approximately six weeks—she went from utter fear of classroom participation to complete immersion. She became such an enthusiastic participant that professors often had to rein her in so others could speak!

Now you might be wondering how generalizable this effect of discovery is. For example, can managers or doctors discover the hidden benefits of delivering bad news? The answer, surprisingly, is yes. One of the doctors in our necessary evils research, in fact, commented on how, in the midst of the discomfort he was feeling when delivering a devastating breast cancer diagnosis to an unsuspecting sixty-year-old patient, he became inspired by the privilege of being able to participate in this intimate moment with the family—which, for him, was part of the essence of the medical profession: "I felt sadness for them, but in the midst of the sadness there was also something inspiring, if that is the correct word. I just felt very privileged and very humbled by the responsibility of sharing this moment with the patient's family . . . being able to share in this exquisitely personal moment, I realized very powerfully once again what a privilege it is to be a physician."

And it wasn't just doctors. Some managers too found a ray of light in otherwise painful and distressing tasks. One manager, for example, started to realize over time that there was a certain professional pride in conducting layoffs "well"—which, for him, meant being able to treat the recipient with dignity and respect: "I realize that it is part of my job. Somebody has to do it. I would rather it be me than most of the people I know. Because I know how to do it with compassion, sensitivity, [and] maintaining dignity."

And as you might also have anticipated, many of the people you've already read about in the book have benefited from this discovery as well once they crossed the thresholds past their comfort zones. That certainly was the case with Annie Jones, who, after getting up the courage to confront Rick Schmitz, discovered that it felt quite empowering to stand up for herself. The worry that, in part, initially blocked Annie from taking the leap—that Rick wouldn't like or respect her—melted away once she got the conviction to give it a try. In the end, taking the chance with Rick allowed Annie to try her hand at being more assertive in other situations as well.

Roger Evans—the banking executive who struggled after moving to a much more collaborative work culture—also experienced a surprising transformation once he loosened the reins and became willing to step outside his comfort zone. Although it did take time for Roger to trust others to do work on his behalf, he slowly started to enjoy the process of collaboration. At the old firm, he was efficient but solitary, and never really developed the skill set to collaborate with others. But at the new firm, Roger not only grew to appreciate the process of collaboration itself—the brainstorming, the back and forth, and, most important, the fact that he could actually rely on the people who worked for him—but also he was pleased to upgrade his professional skill set. It was a very different picture from the frustration and dread he initially experienced upon joining the firm.

The feeling of surprise toward a transformation was also echoed by writer and *Huffington Post* columnist Anniki Sommerville, who wrote a piece about becoming a mom for the first time (or becoming a mum; she's British). Although I'm clearly not a mom (or a mum), I definitely identified with many of the things she mentioned, as I felt many of them too as a first-time dad. Anniki began the piece talking about how, as someone without kids, she had always had a certain degree of disdain for mothers—how they were such a "moany tribe" of "negative automatons," complaining in a joyless way about sleep deprivation and tantrums. But then it happened: Anniki herself became a mom and made certain incredible discoveries about herself in this role—things she thought she'd never enjoy became things she actually did. For example, she loved carrying her daughter on her hip. In her words: "I especially like going to answer the front door with her balanced on one hip. It feels good. Like a cavewoman." She also talked about how having a child helped her discover an adventurous side to herself that she never knew she had: "I hate anything that goes fast. I can't go on a rollercoaster . . . and I have a terrible fear of heights. It's sad because as a child I used to be a real daredevil and enjoyed nothing more than hanging upside down from the climbing frame. But now that I'm spending more time in playgrounds again I've discovered a more adventurous side to myself. I actually love going on a roundabout. And the same goes for the slide. I actually caught myself whooping yesterday. It was a tonic. After a night without sleep."

DISCOVERY #2: I CAN DO THIS (AND I'M BETTER AT IT THAN I THOUGHT)!

I promise that you will never know what you're capable of unless you try.

**Lean In author Sheryl Sandberg
speaking at Barnard College**

Alongside realizing that what you feared all along perhaps isn't as fearful as you had imagined, you may very well discover something else when stepping outside your comfort zone: that you're better at doing the behavior than you originally thought. In fact, decades of psychological research have shown that we're pretty awful at predicting the future—especially about ourselves. We chronically and routinely underestimate our capabilities and our resilience, thinking that we'll feel and be much worse off in the future than we actually end up being. I remember how true this was in my own life when I had my first child. It was in 2004 and I was in the throes of trying to establish myself in my professional career; in particular, I was shooting for the ultimate academic accomplishment—tenure—which is granted to you through a grueling process where your senior colleagues solicit a series of letters about you and your work from ten to twenty experts in your field from around the world. You never see these letters, but they, along with your colleagues' judgment, essentially determine your fate. So, what you can do—and what you need to do—is establish a national and international reputation as a leading thinker in your field. And there's no blueprint for making it happen. You just kind of have to figure it out. Oh—and if you fail, you're fired. You typically have a grace period of a year to find another job, but a negative decision means you must leave the university. So right around this time, in the midst of trying to create this reputation for myself, my first child was born. I was overwhelmed with joy and pride at being a father, but I was equally overwhelmed with the prospect of having to continue this march toward tenure—and, by the way, also teach MBA classes and participate in the service of the university—on two or three hours of sleep and with much less "free" time than I'd ever had in my life. And I was scared.

I honestly didn't think I was going to be able to handle it all—the research, the teaching, the stress, the pressure, or fatherhood, for that matter. But you know what? I did. In fact, with the tremendous support and partnership of my wife, I figured out a way to be a very involved dad, and to get my work done at the same time. And having my daughter, and now a son, in my life has given an entirely different meaning to everything. I started to become much more focused and efficient when doing my work because of how excited I was—and still am—to spend time with my kids and pick them up at school. So, for me, becoming a dad was a perfect example of discovery when stepping outside my comfort zone. I thought it would be a disaster, at least professionally, and frankly it's been quite the opposite.

A very different example of personal discovery from taking a leap comes from Phil Leak, an elementary school principal whose comfort zone challenge involved something fairly unique among the people I interviewed for this book: kissing a pig on the lips. There was a tradition at the school, started by the previous principal, that if the kids at school were able to read more than a certain number of hours during a specially designated "reading month," the principal would do something crazy that the kids would all look forward to. And for the previous principal, who was a pretty outgoing guy—and also clearly not afraid of smooching a swine—the chosen task was to bring an actual pig to school and kiss it on the lips.

Phil was an excellent principal—deeply caring and committed to children and to education, but the idea of doing anything remotely like this was way outside his comfort zone. Not only that, but Phil was an introvert—and also liked being in control. The idea of some out-of-control assembly, with kids screaming and yelling, and then him right there onstage as the center of attention was almost as terrifying as actually puckering up to the pig. The problem, of course, was that as a new principal, he didn't want to do anything to stifle school spirit. And he knew the kids loved the tradition.

So, what was he to do? In the end, Phil used many of the tactics we've talked about in the book. He drew upon his deep sense of conviction that by becoming the center of attention, he would gain the respect of the kids and it would help build the type of community he wanted to build: one where kids are rewarded for hard work and are encouraged to take risks with their learning. If Phil couldn't take the leap outside his own comfort zone, how could he expect his kids to? But pig kissing . . . that still felt like too much, or at least something that was unnecessary to achieve what he wanted.

So, Phil put on his "customization hat" to think of a different way he could achieve the same effect. And then it came to him: a Mohawk! Wouldn't it be awesome to get a Mohawk right in front of everyone—right at assembly? The kids would love it, and it was something that at least felt fathomable. It was outside his comfort zone, for sure, especially the part about being onstage, but he could deal with it. And in the end, it worked like a charm. He got the Mohawk, the kids had a great time, and it became a new tradition at the school.

What Phil realized from this situation was that he could really do this: He could get onstage, be the center of attention, and do something silly. It was definitely outside the realm of his buttoned-up, introverted personality, but interestingly enough, over time, it became a new part of his personality. In fact, Phil described to me how he has learned to become a "temporary extrovert." And he made a point to say that it wasn't faking: Instead, it was authentic. He was able to go into a new, authentic mode where—buoyed by his deep conviction in what he was doing—he could do his version of extraversion that actually felt good. And to Phil, that was the single most surprising thing of all about his experience—not that he was able to get the Mohawk, or live with a Mohawk for a few days, but that he could feel good being outside his comfort zone. That was a complete surprise and something he never anticipated before taking the leap.

This same sense of discovery was true for other individuals you've met in the book. Once Annie Jones took the leap to confront Rick Schmitz, she discovered not only that it wasn't as fearful as she had thought it would be but also that she wasn't half-bad at doing it! Roger Evans discovered that collaboration wasn't rocket science, and that once he gave it a shot and achieved some success with it, he felt much more comfortable giving it a try next time or in other situations. Amanda Nickerson realized it was much easier to have professional conversations with potential job contacts than she ever felt it would be—even after being out of the workforce for so many years and feeling insecure about herself and her professional standing.

When you feel you can do something, you have confidence, or what psychologists call "self-efficacy"—your belief in your ability to succeed in a particular situation. Psychologists call self-efficacy the "can-do cognition." It's like the little train in the book *The Little Engine That*

Could who said "I think I can . . . I think I can" while pulling a much larger train over the mountain. When you take the leap—perhaps driven by a strong sense of conviction and aided by having customized a particular situation to your liking—initial successes that you have can translate into this internal sense of self-efficacy, which becomes a very powerful tool as you continue working on developing a sense of comfort and mastery. In fact, psychological research by Albert Bandura of Stanford University suggests that people with a strong sense of self-efficacy in a particular domain tend to approach challenges confidently, have a deeper interest in the activities they participate in, and recover more quickly from setbacks and roadblocks than those with low self-efficacy. Of course, in the realm of stretching outside your comfort zone, chances are you're likely not going to master whatever your task is right away, but I'll bet you anything that you'll feel a stronger sense of self-efficacy than if you never attempted the task at all. And that alone makes it worth trying.

PART III

How to Make Your New Behavior Stick

We've covered a lot of ground so far. We've learned about the pitfalls of flexing your behavior—and how even considering stretching outside your comfort zone can create such emotional whiplash that many people go to great lengths to avoid doing it altogether. We've looked at the ways you can learn to overcome these challenges by developing a strong sense of purpose or conviction; by learning to tweak, or customize, your behavior; and by developing the clarity necessary to circumvent distorted and exaggerated patterns of thinking. And we've also looked at how, with these tools in place and the courage to take a leap, you can make some pretty amazing discoveries about yourself and about the behavior you've been fearing all along: namely, that it's not as hard as you thought and that you're capable of pulling it off. But one key topic remains: how to make this all stick—how to build the resilience necessary to integrate this challenging new behavior into your more enduring behavioral repertoire. And that's the focus of this final section of the book.

CHAPTER 7

Building Resilience

As she walked up the long path to the most famous country store in all of New Hampshire, Sara Linden had a hard time suppressing her smile. "I can do this," Sara repeated to herself. "The product is good. No one else is selling it. I've got a good shot." And the reality was that she did have a good chance of enticing the store to carry her artisanal goat's milk soap.

A goat farmer by trade, but also a budding entrepreneur on the side, Sara had been working the entire year on perfecting her goat's milk soap recipe. She had sold to friends and family before, and even to her local farmers' market. But this was the big time. She had never even envisaged selling to a store as prestigious as this one, which sold some of New Hampshire's most well-respected artisanal products.

But Sara felt her time had come. The product was great—and in fact had received rave reviews and multiple repeat purchases from people at her local farmers' market, where she had been selling the soap for over a year. And she had also done her homework on this country store: the store itself was legendary in the area, and Sara had gone a few times in recent months to check and make sure there wasn't any competition—in other words, that there was a need for her soap and that no one beat her to the punch.

For Sara, who had previously only sold at farmers' markets, selling to this store was a really big deal. It was like having your antiques featured at Sotheby's or your food at Zabar's. And Sara was ready and even dressed up for the occasion: out with the muck boots, flannel, and jeans and in with a dress, brush, and mascara. Taking a deep breath, Sara opened the squeaky screen door, strutted up to the counter, and plunked her soap on the thick wooden table. "I have some goat's milk soap I'd like to sell in your store!" Sara told the store manager. Her heart was racing. "I really think you'll like this soap," Sara continued. "I know you don't currently carry soap, and I think this could be a nice addition to your offerings." And then she paused, waiting for a response.

"The answer is no," the store manager said without getting up from her seat.

No? Sara thought to herself. She had been rehearsing this situation for weeks and although she of course knew that "no" was a possible response, she hadn't expected it. The hard part was going to be building up the courage to walk through the door and speak to the manager—not having to deal with an actual "no" answer. Sara was flustered.

"Are you sure?" Sara continued, this time with a bit of desperation in her voice. "I have a farm in the town over and we make the soap by hand . . ."

"I don't care if it's goat's milk soap, sheep's milk soap, or llama's milk soap," the manager responded in a way that Sara was completely unprepared for. "The answer is no."

And that was it. Sara thanked the manager for her time, gathered her soap, and went on her way.

In retrospect, Sara might have asked why the manager was so insistent on not purchasing the soap. But in the moment, she was caught off guard and, frankly, overwhelmed. When Sara told me this story, I felt awful hearing it. And so I could imagine that in real life it was just crushing. In fact, I wouldn't have been surprised at all to hear that after this debacle, Sara ended up retreating back to her comfort zone—tending to her goats, selling the occasional bar of soap at the local farmers' market, but never approaching another store again.

But interestingly, that's not what happened. Sara did get the courage to approach another store, and— believe it or not—they bought some soap! It didn't happen immediately, and there certainly were some bumps along the road. But the important point is that Sara didn't give up. In fact, she did quite the opposite: Faced with an obstacle that might very well cause any one of us to retreat, Sara pushed on. And in the end, she felt proud of herself—not only for what happened with this particular vendor but also for her newfound ability to apply this skill going forward.

And the purpose of this chapter is to help you do the same. Most of us can muster up the courage to act outside our comfort zones in a "one-off" situation, but the real trick is making behavior flexing stick: to make it part of our personal repertoires. In the next several pages, we'll look at a series of resources at your disposal for making this happen.

Resource #1: A Thoughtful and Effective Practice Routine

It may sound obvious, but practice is one of the most critical tools in a person's arsenal to integrate a fledgling new skill into one's more permanent bag of tricks. When athletes learn any new skill, such as a new throwing motion or a new way of kicking a soccer ball, they typically practice in less consequential settings first, like in a drill, and then gradually build up to a scrimmage, and then maybe a preseason game . . . and then, ultimately, in a big game. You can take this same analogy and apply it to acting outside your comfort zone.

While practice is critical, it's important to note that the *way* practice is organized and orchestrated is nearly just as critical. Psychologists have found that repeated exposure to *incrementally* challenging situations is the way to go. That is to say, you don't want to expose yourself right away to the most extreme version of a situation you're struggling with—even in practice—since the chances of success are low, and therefore learning will be minimal. You can also become profoundly disappointed and frustrated and, as a result, start looking for ways of avoiding the situation altogether.

Imagine, for example, sending a very promising, but also very novice, rookie baseball player right up to the major leagues. Undoubtedly, he will be excited about the promotion, but his chances of success are extremely small, as evidenced by the many cases of young players trying and then failing at the big league level, sometimes never making it up to that level again. Instead, what's critical is gradual exposure to increasingly challenging situations that meet the criteria of being "just right" for your current level of skill and emotional maturity.

PRACTICE IN SITUATIONS THAT PROVIDE A "JUST RIGHT" CHALLENGE

If you have young children, you will probably recognize the idea of a "just right" book. These are books that are the perfect fit for a child's current reading level—enough to help a child continue building new skills, but not too much to overwhelm. And the same logic applies to practicing for situations outside our comfort zones. We need to find "just right" practice situations to provide us with enough challenge to develop and stretch our skills, but not too much challenge to demoralize us.

Remember Annie Jones, the thirty-four-year-old business development executive at a financial firm whose challenge was finding a way to be assertive and direct with a male portfolio manager who undermined her in client meetings? When we last left her, Annie had been working hard honing her assertiveness skills and had finally gotten the courage to confront Rick Schmitz, the obnoxious and condescending colleague who had humiliated Annie in front of an important client. In the end, after a lot of hard work mustering up the courage to confront Rick, Annie pulled it off. Rick apologized—begrudgingly—and Annie felt extremely proud of herself.

But confidence was often a slippery thing for Annie. She was so proud of herself for standing up to Rick but was worried about whether she could make her assertiveness stick and apply the same strategy to other situations in her work life where she'd really benefit from being more assertive—and there were plenty of them. Despite her great intuition and excellent ideas, Annie was virtually silent at team meetings. As the only woman in the group, and one of the youngest, Annie was always intimidated to say anything for fear others would contradict her (which they probably would) or interrupt her (which they also did all the time). She also had a subordinate, named John, who wasn't pulling his weight, and, Annie believed, was taking advantage of her. So he would be a great candidate to experience Annie's assertiveness as well.

But the question Annie faced was how to make this new assertive style "portable." In other words, how to take what she had learned from the situation with Rick—about how to be more assertive and also about herself and her newfound capabilities—and apply it to other situations. Annie thought she could do it, but she needed a strategy. So Annie put a plan into action.

First she created a "practice schedule." Assertiveness was a skill, Annie had told herself—just like playing tennis, which she loved, or playing bridge, which she loved even more. Annie knew that the more she practiced, the better she'd get and the more confident she'd feel. She also knew from the experience with Rick that the reality of being assertive was *way* less frightening than the anticipation of being assertive. She had been terrified of confronting Rick, but when she finally did it, she realized it wasn't that bad. She didn't want too much time to pass before her next attempt so that her newfound confident perspective wouldn't slip away. That was another reason practice was key.

And speaking of practice, Annie found that it was very useful to practice with a coach, someone who could help her hone her assertiveness skills but also make sure she had the right *attitude* about what she was learning. Annie was a perfectionist and got easily frustrated, especially when learning new skills. As a result, she tended to consider herself a failure when she made mistakes—even if, as a novice, it is completely understandable for her to make them. Annie's coach was tremendously helpful in this regard, helping her adopt what psychologist Carol Dweck calls a "learning orientation," treating mistakes as learning opportunities instead of as a referendum on her lack of skill.

Annie's coach also helped with her continued motivation, reminding her of all the benefits she could achieve by being assertive—and, especially, how good it felt inside to be that way with Rick. It was really helpful to hold on to that confident, proud feeling because that turned out to be the greatest motivation of all to continue. In the end, Annie's efforts paid off. She started participating much more actively in meetings, even really speaking her mind at times. She also took a more proactive approach managing John, her subordinate. John had received approval to work part-time from home, but he wasn't hitting his numbers, and that, of course, reflected poorly on Annie, his manager. Annie had wanted to do something about it for months, but was terrified of saying anything even moderately direct and assertive. But now, inspired by her experience with Rick and her work with her coach, Annie went right at it, speaking her mind: "It seems to me you're working a lot from home, and your numbers are not good. Maybe this isn't the right position for you—and if not, let's address that. But if it is the right position, I need more effort and I need results."

When she was assertive like this, sometimes Annie would do a double take, almost stepping outside her body to hear the words come out of her mouth and then not believing that they were actually hers. But they were—it really was her. And over time, Annie built on the accomplishments with Rick to make assertiveness part of her new default repertoire. In fact, if you met Annie today, you'd be shocked that there ever was an "old" Annie. That's how far she has come.

PRACTICE IN SETTINGS THAT GIVE A REALISTIC PREVIEW OF WHAT YOU'LL ULTIMATELY EXPERIENCE

In addition to providing "just right" training situations that increase in challenge level over time, another critical feature of practice is the ability to craft practice settings that are high in what psychologists call "physical" and "functional" realism: in other words, settings that, ideally, look somewhat like what you will ultimately have to confront in the real world, and, perhaps even more important, function like those settings. Of course, in some situations, like a layoff or delivering a catastrophic medical diagnosis to a patient, it's impossible to simulate the event perfectly, since in any practice environment (even a very realistic one with professional actors playing the role of layoff victim or patient) on some level you will know that the situation is not real, and so the emotions you experience and the other person expresses might not be similar to the ones you'd experience in a real setting.

That caveat aside, it's wise to at least do what you can to increase functional and physical realism in order to increase the chances of your practice translating into successful behavior. And many different organizations and professions do this quite well. The U.S. military, for example, carries out lengthy role-plays in "Hogan's Alley," a highly realistic mock city at the FBI Academy in which trainees carry out a variety of role-play exercises, including hostage negotiation. In medical simulations, functional realism is often created by using an interactive, lifelike mannequin that responds to a learner's

actions in a natural fashion, with responsive eye move-
ments, facial and body gestures indicating pain and discomfort, and physiological reactions consistent with a
real patient.

Realistic training situations are particularly important when the scary situation you're working on isn't
something you do every day. And that is definitely the
case with many of the situations we've already seen in the
book—firings, layoffs, difficult conversations, speeches.
In situations like these, the key is to make the role-play
and practice situations you're doing as realistic as possible—in terms of imagining how the conversation will
unfold as well as what your internal reactions will likely
be—so you can learn the potential script, place yourself
in it, and, ideally, come to realize that you can indeed
tolerate the anxiety and discomfort that you'll ultimately
experience.

In preparing himself to speak publicly about his book
Give and Take (a situation that, at the time, was outside
his personal comfort zone), Adam Grant followed these
principles to a T—constructing a realistic setting to
mimic the conditions he was ultimately going to encounter. Here's how he described the role of practice
in preparing to act outside his personal comfort zone:
"The key is to practice under conditions that resemble

the performance as much as possible. With that in mind, I was surprised to discover that before a talk in front of a crowd of thousands, the best preparation was to practice in front of a small group. In a small group, you can see everyone's facial expressions and feel their gaze burning a hole in your retina."

As Adam's example illustrates, even if you can't mimic the exact situation for which you're preparing (in his case, a talk in front of thousands), you can often find a creative replacement situation. For example, if your ultimate situation is a layoff, you might look for other cases of bad news, such as a difficult performance review, where you can practice and hone your style. Or if you're preparing to speak at a critical board meeting, you might practice speaking up at smaller meetings in your department—again, clearly not mimicking exactly what you're shooting for, but perhaps giving you enough of a realistic preview to ready yourself to deliver the message.

CREATE FORCING MECHANISMS TO "AVOID AVOIDANCE"

To make your behavior change stick, you of course also need to actually go out and do it. I've found that one of the most powerful ways to make this happen is to create these "forcing mechanisms" for yourself—occasions where you have to act outside your comfort zone. Of course, if you're scared of a situation, it's not always so easy to force yourself to do it! So, that's why I've found two "rules" to be particularly useful when crafting forcing mechanisms for yourself: the rule of small commitments and the rule of small steps.

The rule of small commitments is the idea that when you try to force yourself to do something outside your comfort zone, you don't want to bite off more than you can chew; in other words, you don't want your commitment to be so lofty that you will never be able to keep to it. It's like the "just right" rule we talked about earlier with training: You want your commitments to be at the "just right" level as well. For example, let's say that you're afraid of speaking in public but know that, as part of your new job as a division president at your company, public speaking is in your future. What do you do?

You could follow Richard Branson's bold advice: "If somebody offers you an amazing opportunity, but you are not sure you can do it, say yes—then learn how to do it later!" But in certain situations, especially when that unique opportunity is exceedingly far outside your comfort zone, this could be a recipe for failure. That's why "just right" commitments are so essential. If you're afraid of public speaking, one very reasonable forcing mechanism would be to sign up for a public speaking class. You might also commit to a practice speech in front of colleagues at a work lunch. Or if that's too challenging, you might do it over dinner with your family. But make the commitment.

In the mid-1960s psychologists Jonathan Freedman and Scott Fraser did a pioneering study that asked residents of California if they would be willing to put a huge billboard in their front lawns featuring the message "Drive Carefully." As you might imagine, very few were willing to do it. For good measure, a few weeks earlier the researchers had asked a second group of people if they'd be willing to display a three-inch sign with the same message. Since this request was so small, nearly everyone had agreed. What was startling about this experiment was that when the second group (with the three-inch sign) was then asked a few weeks later if they'd be willing to put up a huge billboard, they were three times as likely to say yes, after having acquiesced to the first request.

If you think about it, this has real implications for situations outside your comfort zone. Afraid of delivering bad news? Take a first step of booking a conference room—that's something you can probably easily do.

And then, once you've done that, set up the meeting itself. Or, let's say you're afraid of promoting yourself on social media, even though you know it's critical for your business and career. For a first step, how about finding that domain name and registering it? That's something you can do relatively stress-free, and it's a small commitment that will probably help you ultimately make the bigger one.

Or let's say you are nervous about a speaking opportunity at a company. Take the small step of having a telephone call with the person who is organizing the event. You might find the phone call quite helpful at assuaging your fears; perhaps you'll find out that people at the company have admired your work for a long time and are really hoping that you'll come. It might feel good to be appreciated in this way—and that might increase your motivation enough to take the leap. Or perhaps you'll learn that the speech is at a fancy resort and that you're welcome to bring your family along. That too might ease the tension. The point is that by taking a small step and making a small commitment, you might learn something valuable about the bigger commitment that helps move you outside your comfort zone.

In the end, small steps are critical because they get your foot in the door and grease the skids toward more challenging situations. In part, the reason I'm so passion-ate about this idea of making commitments and creating forcing mechanisms for yourself is the vast number of stories I have heard of people who have taken the leap, endured the challenge, and come out on the other side so much happier than where they started.

Resource #2: A Mind-Set That Supports Learning and Experimentation

Think about the most frustrating and challenging thing you've done in the very recent past—something really outside your comfort zone. For me, it's been housebreak-ing our dog! I am not the most patient person when it comes to things like this, and I also am not particularly skilled at the subtleties of animal psychology. So, when I initially failed in my efforts to train her (and in this case, the failure was pretty obvious) I got frustrated with my-self and thought that I would never be able to do it. Or that I just wasn't a dog person. But of course—given what I'm writing about—I caught myself! I started thinking of how, a long time ago, we did have another dog we housebroke, and I did fairly well with that one. And if my wife and I could learn to "housebreak" two children, a dog was nothing. Once I shifted my mind-set to think about housebreaking as a learning process—and something I would clearly make mistakes with but likely get better at along the way, things got much easier. (Our housebroken dog, by the way, is at my feet as I'm writing this chapter!)

In her outstanding book *Mindset*, Stanford psychologist Carol Dweck distinguishes between two types of mind-sets about learning: a fixed mind-set and a growth mind-set. If you have what Dweck calls a "fixed" mind-set (as in the example above), you tend to see mistakes as evidence of your underlying, innate limitations, as opposed as an inevitable part of the learning process—which would be more of a "growth" mind-set. As you can imagine, when it comes to acting outside your comfort zone, growth mind-sets are the way to go—especially when it comes to making change efforts stick.

But of course, being able to adopt a learning orientation means becoming comfortable with imperfection, which, for many people, is outside their comfort zone. That was definitely the case for Lisa Rose, a relatively new fifth-grade math teacher whose challenging situation was just what we're talking about: becoming comfortable with the fact that on a given day or week or even during a given semester, there will be kids who fall through the cracks and just won't get what you're trying to teach. But Lisa was a perfectionist and also cared deeply about education and helping kids learn. That's why she left a relatively lucrative job in marketing to go into the classroom, where she felt she could make more of a difference. But then she confronted the reality of teaching: She had a pretty unruly group of twenty-five kids—all with different ability levels and learning styles. And many of them simply didn't understand the concepts she was presenting—even after three or four explanations.

Kids failed tests; they failed evaluations; some fell below grade-level standards. Lisa longed to make a difference—and her fledgling self-esteem in this career felt like it was hinging on the external validation of these kids and their ability to grasp the material. Despite how hard she tried, some students just didn't succeed. And Lisa felt awful about it. She felt that she had failed as a teacher and had probably made a wrong career turn.

Over time, however, and with a great bit of peer coaching and encouragement from her more experienced fellow teachers, Lisa started to adopt more of a learning mind-set, which assured that her capacity as a teacher wasn't set in stone, that her skills and perspective would inevitably mature and develop over time, and, perhaps most important, that she had to adopt a more forgiving attitude toward herself. But it certainly wasn't easy.

In the end, if you see failure as evidence of your innate limitations, it becomes self-fulfilling. You end up feeling bad about yourself, and avoid doing the task— or at least putting in only as much effort as before, since, of course, you're limited in the first place. A growth mind-set, on the other hand, is completely different: You make a mistake and see it as part of an overall learning process, which can be quite an advantage when trying to make a new pattern of behavior stick.

NOTICE, APPRECIATE, AND INTERNALIZE YOUR SMALL WINS

Another critical mental tool to have in your arsenal for building resilience around acting outside your comfort zone is your power to notice: to appreciate and internalize what's good and positive and fulfilling about this experience of acting outside your comfort zone, to remember that tinge of pride you felt the first time you did it, or to recall that drop in anxiety once you got into the flow of things. These positive experiences are sources of confidence for the next time around, and can be used to counteract the inevitable anxiety and dread you'll experience, even if you're not a total novice. And what's particularly powerful about these mini epiphanies, or "small wins," is that they come from you—they are *your* experiences. And as psychology research has shown time and time again, it's these intrinsic sources of motivation—as opposed to extrinsic, external rewards—that are particularly powerful, long-lasting, and resilient.

For example, in their terrific book *The Progress Principle*, Teresa Amabile and Steven Kramer find that creative professionals who are able to notice and internalize small wins, or relatively minor but still meaningful accomplishments or experiences, during their everyday working lives, are more engaged in their work and, in the end, better able to achieve their ultimate goals. And in the case of flexing your behavior, these small wins could be achievements of minor goals you've set for yourself, or they could be changes in your internal experience—from dreading something to perhaps not dreading it as much, or even enjoying part of it.

One of the most insightful set of conversations I've

had about the material in this book was with a group of clinical psychologists and cognitive behavioral therapists who do just what we're talking about here for a living—helping people become aware of dysfunctional patterns in their lives and then help them lead happier, more productive, and more fulfilling lives. When I posed the question of how to keep up momentum after you've taken that initial leap, one of them mentioned, without a pause, the critical importance of noticing—and essentially becoming a careful and thoughtful observer of your own personal experiment in behavioral change: Notice when anxiety goes down or is less than you had anticipated. Take note of any positive feelings you do experience when you take the leap. And, especially if the experience is positive—or even more positive than you had anticipated, take heed of that as well.

The pediatric physicians I studied as part of the necessary evils research experienced this effect quite poignantly, especially young doctors who were at the beginning of their tenure. These young doctors hadn't fully internalized the fact that the painful procedures they were performing on young children—and that were making their parents wince in the background—were indeed necessary. Sure, they knew this in theory from lectures they received in medical school, but many of them didn't *feel* the importance. They hadn't yet lived through experiences where painful procedures in the beginning led to successful recoveries in the end.

But once they did have these experiences, it really changed things for them. Noticing what the children—their patients—were gaining from a painful procedure made it exponentially easier to come to grips with the challenges of performing it. Here's how one doctor described this experience: "At the beginning of the year, it was much more distressing to me than it is now. And although I really don't like at all making a child cry, I'm much more at ease just because the information that we get was going to actually benefit them in the future."

And it wasn't just doctors. Many other people I interviewed for this book described a similar effect of how beneficial it was for them to reflect on the benefits of acting outside their comfort zones as a buffer against insecurities they experienced the second or third time around. Roger Evans focused on how good it felt to fit into his new company as he worked hard to keep up his new collaboration skills. And Annie Jones kept the benefits of assertiveness in mind—how empowering it felt and how much of an impact she could have—when trying to keep up the momentum and apply it to other domains of her life.

THINK OF CHANGING BEHAVIOR AS A JOURNEY—AND TAKE HEED OF THE MILE MARKERS ALONG THE WAY

If you like to run or bike, or even walk, and have ever participated in a road race or charity walk, you've undoubtedly seen mile markers along the way, telling you that you're five miles in, for example, and have five miles to go. What's nice about milestones like these is that they give you a real-time sense of your progress. They tell you that you've achieved something: that you've gotten this far. They also tell you how much farther you have to go. And the same is true with learning to act outside your comfort zone. It too unfolds in a series of stages. And when you're in the throes of working hard on adapting your behavior, it's awfully nice to know your mile markers: how far you've come and how far you have to go.

In my work studying and helping people as they learn to stretch beyond their comfort zones, I've found that the process typically happens over a series of five stages. And for many people, it's quite useful to understand these stages as markers of their progression over time. The first stage is the *avoiding stage*, where you aren't acting outside your comfort zone at all. I remember when I first started getting invitations to give talks at corporations outside of the university and it was way outside my comfort zone. I would immediately and reflexively reject these opportunities, rationalizing to myself how they weren't necessary for me to progress in my academic career, or how it wasn't a good use of my time. These excuses were pure avoidance, and becoming aware of this is a critical part of advancing to the next stage in the process, which I call the *considering stage*. At this point, you're toying with the idea, you're thinking about it.

I remember what this was like for me. I'd receive an email asking me to give a talk or do a training session and my anxiety would go sky-high. I'd worry about what it would be like, what I'd possibly say. And I might even start to sketch out on a Word document what my presentation might look like. And although I didn't respond with a yes, I was playing with the idea in my mind, which is certainly progress from the avoidance stage but not quite at the next stage in the process, which is the *attempting stage*—where you pull the trigger and take that leap: You speak up in that meeting; you ask your boss for that raise; you make that phone call or have that discussion. This is where you have stopped avoiding, finished contemplating, and have actually taken the leap. Now, I'm not saying that it's always going to be pretty during the attempting stage. In fact, it often isn't—at least at first. That was definitely the case when I presented for the first time to corporate clients. My presentation was too long, too detailed, and too "academic."

I also remember the first time I spoke up at a faculty meeting as a junior faculty. I thought my heart was going to jump out of my chest it was beating so fast. I was self-conscious, thinking of what I was going to say, scripting it out in my mind, saying it . . . and afterward, realizing that no one had picked up on anything I had said. But I did take the leap, and for me it was a pretty key milestone.

Given the potential for mishaps and missteps, especially early on, during the attempting stage, this territory is rife with backslides. After an unsuccessful try, you might decide you're "no good" at this, or that giving this a try was a "terrible idea." I want to highlight this slippage potential to implore you not to go back down the ladder when you make that inevitable slipup in the *attempting stage*. This stage should be one of experimentation and practice: You're not an expert! You're a novice; you're learning—even if you are older than others who seem to be doing whatever it is with ease, or if you feel hopeless about ever getting it right. Keep at it. Find a mentor or a coach or get feedback from someone you know and trust. My strongest piece of advice at this point in the process is to keep at it—stick with it. Stay in the attempting stage because, over time, as you get a bit of wind at your back and experience under your belt, you can move on to the *refining stage*, where the goal isn't just giving the behavior a shot; it's finding a way to make it your own.

The refining stage is where you truly can work on customizing and personalizing your behavior. In some cases, you're working on refining and perfecting your style. Perhaps some aspects of your style work well, whereas others don't, and you're in the process of doing some "mini experiments," trying out some things, getting feedback, adjusting, and then trying again. At this stage you might also have mastered whatever you're working on in one domain, such as making small talk with colleagues, but there's another domain you haven't yet mastered—say, making small talk with strangers—and so at this refining stage, you're working on a transfer of skill from one arena to another. Either way, though, at this stage you are far more proactive and in control than you were at earlier stages, where the goal may have just been survival, or simply doing whatever behavior it was that you were gearing up to do. At the refining stage, you're perfecting your craft and finding a way to make the behavior your own so you can be simultaneously authentic and effective.

At some point, you may reach the *enjoying stage*, where the behavior has truly become second nature—like muscle memory in sports; it's so ingrained that you don't even think about it. It's like Serena Williams hitting a tennis ball, or Lionel Messi dribbling a soccer ball, or Tom Brady throwing a football. In some ways, I feel that I may have reached this stage with teaching: Initially I was terrified to step into a classroom. I had virtually no experience putting together a lecture, let alone delivering one. It was absolutely terrifying. But because of my job, I couldn't avoid this; it was an essential part of what I was hired to do. So I had to leapfrog to the attempting stage—which might as well have been called "surviving," since that was all I was doing in the first year: trying to stay one class ahead of my students and getting through the semester in one piece. Over time, though, I've had a major personal transformation with my teaching. I have worked hard on my craft and moved from attempting to refining to today, where I might even classify myself as "enjoying." Today teaching is completely second nature. Of course, I still struggle sometimes with a particular lesson, trying to make it as effective and engaging as possible. But I don't really worry about how I'll come across or how to manage the time or how to connect and engage with students because it's become pretty automatic and natural for me now.

So, next time you're in the throes of a challenging situation of your own, don't consider yourself a failure if you still struggle to get your situation right . . . or if you're still trying to figure out how to make whatever it is you're working on into something that feels like your own. My hope, actually, is that instead of beating yourself up, you can realize that learning to act outside your comfort zone is a process—and one that takes time, effort, strategy, and patience—and that you may only be at the attempting stage with your situation, but that is quite a milestone given where you've come from. As I mentioned before, you can even consider the realization that you're avoiding something you'd love to stop avoiding a pretty significant breakthrough. The idea of a journey or a process, I hope, can help put into perspective the challenges and difficulties you're experiencing along the way.

Finally, we all have our own private "portfolios" of situations outside our comfort zones that we're working on . . . and we're often at very different stages in each of these different journeys. For me, MBA or undergraduate teaching at Brandeis is something I feel is probably in the enjoying stage, but would that be the case if I took a job at another university with very different students and expectations in the classroom? Or how about teaching to executives? Here, I am probably in the refining stage: working on my craft rather than being able to produce on relative autopilot.

And in yet other types of situations, I might be in the attempting stage or even the avoiding stage, where I know I may be avoiding something that would be good for me, but I can't quite get myself to take the plunge. And what's nice about thinking about the range of situations in your portfolio is that you can sometimes ride the coattails of confidence you have in one domain while struggling with something in another domain. You can reflect on your sense of pride and accomplishment over having mastered interviewing, and use some of that positive energy to help you take the next steps in your attempts to network. Or, alternatively, your success at speaking up in small meetings can be motivation to work even harder on other situations you might find challenging at work, like presenting in front of your colleagues, or pitching an idea to the boss.

Resource #3: A Healthy Support System

Very few of us in life go at anything completely alone, and that's especially true in the case of stretching outside our comfort zones. Others help us; they inspire us; they provide us with strategies to get where we want to go as well as the inspiration and courage to make it happen. That was certainly true for most of the people you've read about in this book. Take Sara Linden, the soap maker from New Hampshire, for example. If Sara had gone at this all alone—if she lived alone on the goat farm, had no family, no friends, no one to help pick her up and encourage her to continue acting outside her comfort zone, it's pretty likely she never would have set foot in a store again, because the experience of rejection was just that crushing for her.

But luckily, like many of us, Sara did have a family and friends and people to mentor and coach her, and provide her with just enough encouragement—and accountability—that she was able to get back in the game and start trying to sell more soap. For Sara, it was her husband, James, who corrected her "doomsday" procla-mations about how no one would ever buy her soap and how she was a "complete failure." And then her dear friend Lucy, a fellow farmer with her share of failed efforts at selling products as well, who also provided essential feedback and guidance. Rejections were just part of the process, Lucy explained. It was like baseball: You're considered an outstanding hitter if you succeed only three out of ten times—and in sales, it was a similar story. You never know what's going to happen the next time around and the only way to find out is to give it a try. Buoyed by her husband's clarity and her friend's conviction, Sara did find the courage to try again at a slightly smaller local store, and came away smiling with a purchase order in hand. And this same theme is true for many others as well.

Roger Evans, the hard-driving executive who struggled collaborating with others, worked with a professional coach who videotaped him during meetings at the firm so he could see evidence of what others had complained about. In fact, it was through these videotaped sessions with a coach that Roger had his biggest aha moments—where he could see quite clearly what others were talking about—and the impression it made on them. For example, he could see that after he took charge of a meeting or shut down a conversation, people would become silent or productivity would grind to a halt—and actually seeing that became a critical piece of "data" and inspiration to start making a change.

Another example of someone who greatly benefited from a mentor when stretching outside her comfort zone was Ella Cheng, the college sophomore running for student office but terrified of what she had to do to win the seat. Eventually, Ella was able to gain the courage to go door to door and have conversations with potential voters—and discovered that she actually *liked* many aspects of having these conversations. But what I didn't mention when I told the original story was that Ella had a secret weapon in the early days to help make this work: a fellow student leader and friend who went along with Ella on the first several conversations with potential voters. It was her friend who convinced Ella that she didn't need to promote herself to voters, but instead to have honest conversations with them about their challenges at school and how student government might help to address them. And that tip alone ended up being the most critical one for Ella because it allowed her to be herself and start to enjoy the conversations.

In my own life, I've been blessed with several important mentors: my graduate school advisor Richard Hackman, whom I've mentioned before, and Joel Brockner, a professor at Columbia University who taught me as a twenty-year-old and inspired me to go into the organizational behavior field. But perhaps my greatest mentor has been my own father. My father has always been there for me when I've had to step outside my professional comfort zone. When I was learning to write in high school (and it's funny to look back on that now), it was my dad who stopped whatever he was working on to take a look and be my writing coach. When I took a year off from college to live in Paris and discovered this passion of studying how people were acting outside their cultural comfort zones in business situations abroad, it was my dad who I excitedly faxed (yes, it was that long ago!) from Paris, so curious to name what I was so passionate about but uneasy about what it meant for potentially changing my career path.

And at each step along the way as an academic—from starting my PhD to doing my dissertation to teaching for the very first time, and now, reinventing myself as much more of a public person writing for a general audience—he's been there for me as well, advising me when I'm insecure about what I'm saying or doing. Teaching for the first time? No problem—he had already been teaching for thirty years when I taught my first class and was a great source of confidence and concrete advice when I had to step into a classroom for the very first time. Writing a book? Yup, he had done that too—many times, in fact. Giving a speech? Yes, that too—or having to be on the radio or television or reading drafts of things before I'd ever share them with anyone else. And from reading about the experiences of people across professional contexts, I know I'm not alone in having someone special to help me as I stretch outside my comfort zone.

Some people have a hard time asking for help—especially people who feel that they're imposters to begin with and that by asking for help, they'll somehow be "found out" and the truth will be told. If this is you, do your best to realize that asking for help and feedback is a strength, not a weakness. And I hope that from having read this book, you'll see that everyone in some way struggles acting outside their comfort zones. So it's only smart to use the resources at your disposal—like a mentor—to help along the journey.

Early on in her career, General Motors CEO Mary Barra's mentor helped her to become more vocal at meetings. Steve Jobs's early career mentor Robert Friedland helped him learn to be more assertive and take charge of situations, when he initially was a very quiet, private, and self-effacing person. And Richard Branson's mentor, Freddie Laker, helped him overcome a fear of public

speaking. But I want to emphasize that you don't necessarily always need a once-in-a-lifetime mentor to make
this work. You can cobble together mentoring from multiple sources: feedback and advice from a colleague—or
even from a seminar or a book or a magazine. You can
get psychological support from friends or family. And
you can ask people you're close with—friends, family, a
support group—to hold you accountable for your efforts
at personal transformation: to help you notice and cele-
brate even the tiniest of accomplishments while also
pointing out slippage back to the comfort zone. The
point isn't to find the perfect mentor; it's to recognize
that everyone needs mentor-*ing*—and to piece that together from multiple places.

In the end, making a stretch beyond your comfort
zone is a choice, and one you should consider thoughtfully. But one thing should be clear: Magic can happen
in a lot of places—not just outside your comfort zone.

CHAPTER 8

The Myths and Realities

We've covered a lot of territory in this book. We've discussed why it can be so challenging to act outside our comfort zones, how we so often avoid doing it, and how, through hard work, strategy, and persistence, we can learn to grow and develop in ways we might never have thought possible. Along the way, we've met a multitude of professionals who have shared their stories and experiences—and in doing so, have hopefully inspired you to take a leap in your own life.

But I'd be remiss ending here, without talking a bit about all the hype that exists out there about comfort zones, because it's clearly in the zeitgeist. There has been a lot written about comfort zones, and frankly, I believe that much of it is false, or at least misguided. If you pay attention to the hype and rhetoric, you'll notice that most people seem to say that acting outside your comfort zone is actually pretty easy to do—just grit your teeth and take that leap, or (my favorite) just "suck it up." But as we've learned, stretching beyond your comfort zone takes far more than just "sucking it up." And in fact, there are times when it's probably not such a good idea to take the leap in the first place. So, in the spirit of debunking the myths and ending with a few key takeaways, I'd like to give you a sense of what I see as five key myths and realities about acting outside your comfort zone. See if you agree.

> **Myth #1:** All it takes to step outside your comfort zone is taking a leap.
>
> **Reality:** Very few people spontaneously "leap" outside their comfort zones; rather, that leap is the result of considerable thinking and deliberation.

For most people I've talked with—and also from my own experience—gathering the courage to take a leap doesn't typically happen in an instantaneous flash; a lightbulb doesn't suddenly appear over your head, inspiring you to say, "Yes! I do have to go network!" or "Of course—small talk is definitely in my wheelhouse!" Instead, it often comes from a slow and steady progression of very small steps over time—and usually steps that don't actually involve performing the behavior yourself. Instead, you might be observing the behavior, or imagining yourself performing the behavior, or working internally on the courage to eventually perform the behavior. And then—it happens. You do it. And to the outside it might feel like an instantaneous transformation, but you know the truth: At some point, you had nudged yourself enough, gotten yourself just to the brink of being willing to give it a go, and then something pushed you over the edge.

In fact, I suspect that when people hear messages like "Just take that leap!" or "Life begins outside the comfort zone!" people become discouraged rather than inspired. But beware of drawing any conclusions from what you observe from the outside, because what seems like an easy and effortless performance may very well be something that person struggles with inside—perhaps even quite a bit. That's been the case for me countless times when I've presented in public. People have told me I seem fully at ease, when inside I felt like I was going to vomit or faint. And from hearing countless stories of others learning to stretch their own behavior in a myriad of ways, I know this to be true.

> **Myth #2:** The "magic" only happens outside your comfort zone.
>
> **Reality:** The "magic" can happen both inside and outside your comfort zone.

If you take a quick look at Google Images under the topic "comfort zone," you'll realize something very quickly: Comfort zones really get a bad rap. One picture portrays the comfort zone as being a "dull life" or "just getting by." In others, the comfort zone is about "depression," "fear," or "mediocrity." And then of course, you have the famous picture with the two bubbles I described earlier: your comfort zone and "where the magic happens," with the implication that if "magic" is ever going to happen, it's definitely not happening in your comfort zone.

But is that always true? Is it never a good thing to stay in your comfort zone?

What if, for example, you just don't have it in you? You're too emotionally exhausted, for example, or overwhelmed, and the likelihood of success is incredibly low. For example, I remember, quite well, toying with the idea of doing more consulting and writing for businesses earlier in my career—which at the time represented a major shift outside my comfort zone. But the problem was timing: I was struggling to get tenure and was swamped with research work. I also was learning to teach for the first time in an MBA program. And, finally, my wife and I had just had our first child and my wife was expecting our second. I was running on four hours of sleep a night, having bizarre delirious moments in class, wondering if I had just said what I thought I said, and on more than one occasion thinking halfway through a lecture that there was no way I was going to make it to the end. I wanted to make this stretch—and, in fact, had gotten into academics in the first place primarily as a means to make a difference in the world beyond the ivory tower. But this clearly couldn't happen then—I needed to use the limited time and energy that I did have to focus on achieving the goal of tenure. And so I stayed within my comfort zone of academic research and writing—that is, until I had more time, energy, and freedom to experiment.

Another time when it might make sense to stay within your comfort zone is when there's someone else more capable than you are to perform a particular task—*and* your team faces time pressure to achieve an important goal. A good example from a story you've already heard is Dan Gold, the carwash entrepreneur who loved developing software to run car washes more efficiently but felt awkward and uncomfortable pushing his product and trying to make a sale. Dan could have applied the techniques I discuss here in the book to learn to stretch outside his comfort zone, but there were two big problems: First, he wasn't passionate at all about sales—and so he didn't have that critical sense of conviction to make the leap. And second, his company was under severe time pressure: There were only a certain number of car washes needing computer software and so the person who got to them first would seal the deal. So, instead of waiting for Dan to learn to stretch his fledgling skills, he did the far more expedient thing and hired a salesperson.

And if you look at some of the greatest partnerships in history, that's exactly how they're structured: People with complementary skills coming together to form a whole greater than the sum of its parts. For example, Apple in the early days was a partnership, with Steve Wozniak's technical skills paired with Steve Jobs's business foresight and design savvy. Similarly, it's been said that Dave Packard's business sense was a perfect complement to William Hewlett's expertise with technological innovation. Of course, you don't want to use the idea of complementary skills as an excuse for always staying within your comfort zone and outsourcing anything difficult, but in certain cases—especially where your motivation to change is low, and time pressure is high— it makes all the sense in the world to stay with what you're good at and have someone else do what you're not.

Finally, sometimes the magic actually does happen inside your comfort zone—or slightly outside. It's your sweet spot, the place where you have just the right amount of skill to have the experience of "flow" when performing a task—which, according to psychologist Mihaly Csikszentmihalyi, means losing track of time, not thinking or worrying about yourself, and being fully immersed in what you're doing.

Edward Fenster, cofounder and chairman of Sunrun,

a company providing solar energy to homeowners, put it well: "To stay engaged and happy, I need to operate slightly outside my comfort zone. If I get too far I become incompetent, and things can fall apart. If I stay too safely within my comfort zone, I get bored."

The overall lesson here, though, is to pick your spots. Stay in your comfort zone in certain situations; move slightly outside in others; and sometimes, when the circumstances are right: take that big leap.

Myth #3: I'm the only one who struggles with situations outside my comfort zone.

Reality: Nearly everyone struggles with situations outside their comfort zones.

In many ways, it's been quite easy to research this book—at least in terms of collecting stories from people about acting outside their comfort zones, mostly because nearly everyone seems to have a story—and for most people, it's more than one. In fact, when I mention the topic of this book—that this is about why acting outside our comfort zones is so hard, how we avoid doing it, and what we can do about it—people typically smile and nod with a knowing look on their face. "Do I have a story for you!" they sometimes say, and then proceed to tell me about their struggles with networking, or making small talk, or giving speeches, or being assertive, or whatever the situation happens to be. I have been struck both by how many people have a story to tell and also how comfortable many people are to share their stories.

This idea of acting outside your comfort zone is a pretty universal phenomenon—in life, but also in the stories we know and love from literature and film. It's called the "hero's journey": a pattern of narrative originally identified by scholar Joseph Campbell, where a "hero" leaves his or her familiar world behind and learns to navigate an unfamiliar world, often leaping into the unknown, being "tested," confronting their greatest fear, and then returning home a changed person—often in ways they didn't expect. And if you think about it, some of the most memorable characters and stories from modern and ancient literature follow this exact format. It's a core theme in *The Odyssey*, *The Hobbit*, *Star Wars*, and many other classic stories of adventure.

These stories are all about vulnerability, about courage, about taking a chance, and about learning something you never would have necessarily predicted. And for us—who are not fictional characters—we have the opportunity to craft our own stories, to write our own hero's tale. If you face a situation like networking, or making small talk, or speaking up at meetings, or confronting something at work or at home, what story are you going to write for yourself? Are you going to get the courage to take that leap? And might you have the opportunity to learn something about yourself from doing something outside your comfort zone but something you deeply believe in or that you know is important for your personal or professional development? As authors of our own stories, we have the unique opportunity to craft our own endings.

We know our struggles and perhaps assume that they have everything to do with us, attributing our challenges to our own personalities or characters or lack of ability—as opposed to the situation of being away from home, having to present in front of an audience, or whatever the particular challenge might be. You just happen to have intimate "backstage" access to your experience and only a peripheral, "front stage" view of other people's struggles. My hope is that by sharing so many people's stories in this book—"regular" people like you and me, and also public figures who have written or spoken poignantly about their own challenges—you'll be able to "normalize" your own reactions, realizing that if you struggle, it's typical rather than unique, and that with the tools and techniques described in this book, you can learn to take action despite these challenges and get yourself on a positive trajectory.

> **Myth #4:** Getting out of your comfort zone is just about "sucking it up."
>
> **Reality:** "Sucking it up" is important, but so too are other strategies, which, in fact, can ultimately make "sucking it up" less necessary.

In doing research for this book, I can't tell you how many people (mainly men) told me that their "strategy" for dealing with situations outside their comfort zones was to just "suck it up." Some offered a slightly more graphic term, but the essence was the same: You're in a situation where you have to perform and it's out of your comfort zone? Just suck it up—or, translated into psychology speak, don't let your emotions guide your behavior. Let the logical, sensible, strategic side of you dictate the action. For example, if you fear public speaking but know you need to speak in a certain situation, you do need to deal with the fear you experience, because if you don't, fear might take control of the wheel and drive you right out of the room. However, here's the thing: Sucking it up—or suppressing emotion—is sometimes necessary. But it's not the only strategy in our arsenal, and it's definitely not what getting outside our comfort zones is all about. In fact, if you follow the guidelines in this book, there should ideally be less stress to have to "suck it up." If you achieve clarity in your thinking (reconciling cognitive distortions and normalizing exaggerated thinking), if you can find a way to achieve that sense of purpose and conviction about the reasons you're taking this action—even if it's against the grain of what you'd naturally and comfortably do—and if you can customize and personalize your behavior so that it actually feels more natural, there will be less to suck up. You'll feel more in control, more comfortable, and less stressed overall. So a key overall takeaway and important message to the "suck it uppers" out there:

Don't remove the tool from your arsenal, but realize that there's a great deal more you can do before having to take that particular tool out of your tool belt.

> **Myth #5:** With enough inspiration, anyone can stretch outside their comfort zone.
>
> **Reality:** Anyone can do it, but it takes more than inspiration; it takes effort, persistence, strategy, and a keen understanding of the challenges.

It's true that anyone can take the leap and step outside their comfort zone. Or at least I feel that way from witnessing and learning about the successful experiences of so many people in so many different challenging situations. But there's an important caveat: Stepping out of your comfort zone isn't magic; it takes time and effort and persistence to take the leap and make it stick. People return home early from studying abroad. They try to speak in a meeting, have a bad experience, and never speak again. That's why it's so critical to use what we talked about here in the book to increase the odds of making this stick. If you can find a way to make the behavior your own—to customize and personalize it so that it feels that much more natural and comfortable to you, and if you're able to find a way to practice in "just right" situations, find a mentor or a colleague who can provide informational and psychological support, and all the other things that increase the odds of making it stick—you can avoid "one hit wonder" status and really make behavior flexing part of your personal repertoire. But it's not just about taking that leap. It's creating the conditions so that the initial leap has staying power and becomes part of your own personal repertoire.

You've spent your entire life stretching outside your comfort zone. As a toddler, you moved from the comfort of crawling on the floor to the terror of walking on two feet—by yourself. You left home for preschool and then elementary school and then, eventually, to the freedom of middle school, high school, and college. You took a leap when you moved from college to your first professional job. You probably then changed roles at that job—or even changed jobs or careers. You may have moved from being single to being in a relationship—and perhaps married. And then for most people, having kids is stretching way outside their comfort zones! So, the next time you face a situation outside your comfort zone—whether it's speaking up or backing down, asking for a raise or raising a point in a meeting—remember that in many ways, this is all old hat. You've done this your entire life, and you can do it again.

Getting outside your comfort zone is not easy. It takes time, effort, strategy, and determination. But with a solid plan in place and the courage to take it forward, your results can be extraordinary.

PART IV

Practical Tools: Applying *Reach* to Your Own Life

You've had a chance to hear how others have grappled with situations outside their comfort zones. Now it's your turn to apply some of these tools to your situation.

Start by selecting a particular situation that is outside your personal comfort zone. Your situation might be:

At Work:

- Speaking up at a meeting
- Promoting yourself during an informational interview, conference, or job fair
- Making small talk at a conference or by the watercooler
- Giving negative feedback
- Following up with a manager who has not responded to your request
- Asking someone for help

At Home

- Having a difficult conversation with a friend, spouse or partner, or parents
- Making small talk at a party where you don't know anyone
- Confronting a parent whose child is bullying yours

These are just examples. Yours can be any situation where you need to act outside your comfort zone to be effective.

Name Your Situation

My situation is:

_____

_____

_____

_____

_____

Next, answer the questions below and use the following scoring system to arrive at your answer.

1 = Strongly agree

2 = Agree

3 = Neutral

4 = Disagree

5 = Strongly disagree

Competence Challenge Self-Assessment

____1. I'm not very good at performing the task required in this situation.

____2. I don't feel confident performing this task.

____ Your combined Competence Challenge score

Authenticity Challenge Self-Assessment

____1. This behavior feels unnatural to me.

____2. I don't feel genuine performing this behavior.

____ Your combined Authenticity Challenge score

Resentment Challenge Self-Assessment

____1. I feel that it's unfair that I have to accommodate my behavior in this situation.

_____2. I feel resentful about having to change my style.

_____ Your combined Resentment Challenge score

Likeability Challenge Self-Assessment

_____1. I worry that people won't like me when I change my behavior in this situation.

_____2. I'm afraid I'll turn people off when I change my behavior in this situation.

_____ Your combined Likeability Challenge score

Morality Challenge Self-Assessment

_____1. I have serious concerns about the morality of this behavior.

_____2. When I perform this behavior, I worry about whether I'm being ethical.

_____ Your combined Morality Challenge score

Your Overall Portfolio of Personal Challenges

Take a quick look at your scores. On which dimensions do you face the highest level of challenge? Which dimensions aren't as challenging for you?

Your Greatest Challenges (circle one or more):

Competence   Authenticity   Resentment

Likeability   Morality

**Aspects That Aren't So Challenging
(circle one or more):**

Competence   Authenticity   Resentment

Likeability   Morality

What Are Your Avoidance Strategies?

It's perfectly natural to do whatever you can to avoid acting outside your comfort zone. We all do it! However, as a result of doing this, we also often limit our learning and growth and become less effective than we could be at our jobs.

So in the spirit of self-discovery, let's take a look at the specific ways you might limit yourself by examining four of the most common avoidance strategies. You can use the same situation or task you've been considering thus far, or a different one.

Name Your Situation

Examples:

1. Going to a networking event

2. Having a difficult conversation with my colleague

Your situation:

_____

_____

_____

_____

_____

_____

Next, let's take a look at four of the most common avoidance strategies that people use. Do any of these ring a bell for you? Remember to be honest with yourself.

1. AVOID THE TASK ENTIRELY

Are there any times you structure your life or job to avoid doing this task altogether—even though it could be critical for your job and career?

I use this strategy:

Often   Sometimes   Rarely

Examples

1. I know networking events could really help my career and business, but I just hate talking with people I don't know . . . so I end up going to very few of them, if any.

2. I know I should have difficult conversations with my colleague, but they're just too stressful, so I avoid them.

Your situation:

_____

_____

_____

_____

_____

_____

---

2. DO THE TASK ONLY PARTWAY

Do you ever only do this challenging task partway, perhaps doing the part that's slightly more comfortable and avoiding the rest?

I use this strategy:

Often   Sometimes   Rarely

Examples

1. Because I feel so uncomfortable at networking events, I typically only go for a few minutes at the very beginning and then pretend I have somewhere else to go.
2. Because of how uncomfortable difficult conversations are for me, I tend to discuss only part of what's bothering me, or address only the issues that are easiest to talk about.

Your situation:

_____

_____

_____

_____

_____

_____

3. PROCRASTINATE

Do you ever stall while attempting to perform this task, and as a result either miss a key deadline, or do it too late to have the most positive effect?

I use this strategy:

Often   Sometimes   Rarely

Examples

1. Because I feel so uncomfortable at networking events, I rarely respond to invitations and often put networking on the back burner.

2. I often put off having difficult conversations, rationalizing to myself that it's not the "right time," when in reality, I'm just procrastinating.

Your situation:

_____

_____

_____

_____

_____

_____

4. PASS THE BUCK (AND HAVE SOMEONE ELSE DO IT)

Do you ever ask or assign someone else to carry out what needs to be done because it's too uncomfortable for you to do, thereby avoiding the task, but in the process limiting your own learning and growth?

I use this strategy:

Often   Sometimes   Rarely

Examples

1. Because I feel so uncomfortable at networking events, I often get my assistant to attend them for me (even though I probably should be the one representing the business).
2. I sometimes get someone else to talk with my colleague instead of me since I'm so uncomfortable doing it myself.

Your situation:

_____

_____

_____

_____

_____

_____

Unlocking Your Sources
of Personal Conviction

Ask yourself this question: If you didn't experience any anxiety at all in your chosen situation—if it were completely comfortable and stress-free—would it be something you'd *like* to be able to do? Would it be exciting? Would it help your career? Would it help your self-confidence? The answers to these questions can help reveal your potential sources of conviction—why, for you, it might very well be worth taking that leap and stretching outside your comfort zone.

So let's take a look at a few potential sources of conviction.

You can evaluate each possibility by using the same scale as before:

1 = Strongly agree

2 = Agree

3 = Neutral

4 = Disagree

5 = Strongly disagree

Potential Source of Conviction #1: Respect

_____1. Doing this behavior will make me look good in other people's eyes.

_____2. Doing this behavior will win people's respect (or a particular person's respect).

_____ **Your combined score for Respect**

Potential Source of Conviction #2: Skill Development

_____1. Doing this behavior will help me develop skills I don't currently have.

_____2. Doing this behavior will help me improve existing skills.

_____ **Your combined score for Skill Development**

Potential Source of Conviction #3: Career Advancement

_____1. Doing this behavior will increase my chances for promotion.

_____2. Doing this behavior will help me move up the career ladder.

_____ **Your combined score for Career Advancement**

Potential Source of Conviction #4: Boosting Your Self-Esteem

____1. Doing this behavior will make me feel proud of myself.

____2. Doing this behavior will boost my self-esteem.

____   Your combined score for Boosting Your Self-Esteem

Potential Source of Conviction #5: Helping Others

____1. Doing this behavior will help me contribute to a cause I care about.

____2. Doing this behavior will help me make a difference in others' lives.

____   Your combined score for Helping Others

Which of the potential sources of conviction received the highest score for you?

Is there another potential source of conviction for you that is not on this list?

Learning to Customize Your Behavior

One of the best ways of making your new behavior feel more natural and comfortable is to make it your own. Customize it: Put your own personal spin on the behavior so it feels authentic to you but also still effective and appropriate. Below you will see five different potential tools you can use to customize your behavior. See if any of them apply to you and your situation.

CUSTOMIZABLE ELEMENT #1: YOUR DIALOGUE

These are *your* words—what *you* actually say. And you will find that there are many ways you can make minor adjustments to what you actually say so that it feels slightly more comfortable and natural for you.

For example:

- If you're terrified of speaking up in meetings, you might learn a few catchphrases to get people's attention, such as: "Have we thought about this?" or "Here's another idea we might consider."
- If you have to deliver difficult news and are afraid,

you might script out the first few sentences of your message.

- If you feel awkward making small talk in social settings, you might think of a few relevant topics ahead of time, or work on a few conversation starters that you know you're comfortable talking about.

Can you think of ways to customize your dialogue to make behavior flexing more comfortable for you?

If so, jot down an example for yourself.

_____

_____

_____

_____

_____

_____

CUSTOMIZABLE ELEMENT #2: YOUR BODY LANGUAGE

Another lever you have for increasing your level of comfort is your nonverbal behavior—your posture, your eye contact, your smile, your tone of voice, and the way you sit or stand or walk.

For example:

- When mustering up the courage to speak up at a meeting, you might stand up tall, lean forward with your hands slightly at your sides, and plant your hands firmly on the desk.
- When having a difficult conversation with a partner or spouse, you might make sure not to have a "closed" or "defensive" body posture—like with your legs or arms crossed—so that you appear open to listening and hearing the other person's perspective.

> Can you think of ways to customize your body language to make behavior flexing more comfortable for you?
>
> If so, jot down an example for yourself.

_____

_____

_____

_____

_____

CUSTOMIZABLE ELEMENT #3: TIMING

In certain circumstances, timing is another variable under your control—and that might mean the timing of the situation itself, as in when it occurs, or also the time and pacing of your behavior within the situation.

For example:

- If you know you're going to be stressed having to deliver bad news to someone, you might choose a time to do it when you feel most capable—perhaps after a long run, or sandwiched between activities you enjoy and that give you energy.
- If you dread networking events with lots of people, you might purposefully come a few minutes early so you can get your confidence flowing with only a few people in the crowd.

Acknowledging that you don't always have complete control over time, can you think of ways to customize timing to make behavior flexing more comfortable for you?

If so, jot down an example for yourself.

_____

_____

_____

_____

_____

CUSTOMIZABLE ELEMENT #4: PROPS

In theater, you bring props to the show—items that you carry with you as you execute your role. The same is true in organizations.

For example:

- You might wear your favorite "power suit" when you know you need to be assertive.
- If you're about to make a big presentation, you might wear your "lucky" ring, or something else that makes you feel courageous.

- If you are uncomfortable giving critical feedback to a colleague, you might bring your notes with you, or even aspects of the work you wanted to give feedback about.

> Can you think of any "props" you could integrate into your situation to make behavior flexing more comfortable for you?
>
> If so, jot down an example for yourself.

CUSTOMIZABLE ELEMENT #5: THE CONTEXT

Finally, in certain cases, you can customize the context—or your position or role in that context—to maximize comfort and performance.

For example:

- If you're afraid of participating in a classroom discussion, you might sit in the front row so the class seems smaller.
- If you're afraid of going to a networking event, you might bring a supportive colleague, especially if

you sense that having them there will make you feel more relaxed and confident.

Can you think of ways to customize the context for your situation?

If so, jot down an example for yourself.

_____

_____

_____

_____

_____

_____

Developing Clarity

When taking on a job or a task outside our comfort zones, our thinking patterns can become our worst enemy. We can become fixated and obsessed by worst-case scenarios, and also by best-case scenarios, when the reality is somewhere in between.

Can you think of a situation where you've experienced this kind of exaggerated, polarized thinking?

Here's an example: You're asked to take on your first major leadership responsibility. You're honored to be asked, but stressful thoughts immediately flood your mind in the form of "worst case" and "best case" thinking:

"Worst Case" Thinking

I'll feel awkward and unnatural leading meetings and telling people what to do. I'm afraid it will feel intolerable. I'll feel overwhelmed. I won't be able to make sense of my responsibilities or do them successfully. I'll feel trapped in a job that feels like something I didn't sign up for. People will hate me since I'll be the one making tough calls and mediating conflicts.

"Best Case" Thinking

This job will be a perfect fit for me right away. I'll succeed immediately and be seen as a leadership "prodigy." Everyone will love and respect me and I'll handle conflict with ease.

The antidote to this distorted thinking is clarity: the ability to take that middle-ground approach and "normalize" your thinking about the most *realistic* scenario.

Realistic Thinking

I'll feel natural at times—and at other times probably less so. I'll have to grow into the role over time. I'll have some successes and some failures. The job will be a learning experience. There may be moments of resentment, but I imagine I'll also enjoy aspects of the job. Some people will really like me, and others won't as much . . . but that's just part of the job.

How about you? Can you try this out for a situation of your own?

Name Your Situation

_____

_____

_____

Your Worst-Case Thinking

_____

_____

_____

Your Best-Case Thinking

_____

_____

_____

Your Realistic Thinking

_____

_____

_____

Notes

Introduction

5 **something that looks like this:** "Image of comfort zone," accessed June 5, 2016, http://www.huffingtonpost.com/jacob-morgan/why-getting-out-of-your-c_b_6660452.html.

9 **what my research collaborator:** The research about necessary evils that I profile in this book was done collaboratively with Joshua Margolis from Harvard Business School.

Chapter 1. Why Reaching Outside Your Comfort Zone Is So Hard

25 **"I know I am not a real CEO":** "Startups Anonymous: A List of Fears from the CEO of a Startup in NYC." Accessed June 5, 2016, https://pando.com/2014/03/12/startups-anonymous-a-list-of-fears-from-the-ceo-of-a-startup-in-nyc.

30 Quotation from my own research data for necessary evils field research project, 2003–2008.

30   **Recent studies in neuroscience:** Lieberman, Matthew D. *Social: Why Our Brains Are Wired to Connect*. New York: Crown, 2013.

35   Quotation from my own research data.

37   **Barbra Streisand:** Stossel, Scott. "Performance Anxiety in Great Performers: What Hugh Grant, Gandhi, and Thomas Jefferson Have in Common." *Atlantic*, January/February 2014, accessed June 5, 2016, http://www.theatlantic.com/mag azine/archive/2014/01/what-hugh-grant-gandhi-and-thom as-jefferson-have-common/355853.

37   **Adele:** Touré, "Adele Opens Up About Her Inspirations, Looks, and Stage Fright." *Rolling Stone*, April 28, 2011, accessed June 5, 2016, http://www.rollingstone.com/music/news/adele -opens-up-about-her-inspirations-looks-and-stage -fright-20120210.

37   **Arianna Huffington:** "Arianna Huffington's Tips for Handling That 'Obnoxious Roommate' in Her Head." *Huffington Post*, March, 26, 2014, accessed June 6, 2016, http://www.huff ingtonpost.com/2014/03/25/arianna-huffington-advice -obnoxious-roommate_n_5030116.html.

37   **Reese Witherspoon:** "Witherspoon Hoped She Wouldn't Win Oscar." *Express*, November 27, 2008, accessed June 6, 2016, http://www.express.co.uk/celebrity-news/73144/Wither spoon-hoped-she-wouldn-t-win-Oscar.

38   **This was certainly the case for Scott Stossel:** Stossel, Scott. *My Age of Anxiety: Fear, Hope, Dread, and the Search for Peace of Mind*. New York: Knopf, 2014.

39   **Take, for example, Natalie Portman:** "Natalie Portman Harvard Commencement Speech," accessed June 5, 2016, https:// www.youtube.com/watch?v=jDaZu_KEMCY.

40   **Jodie Foster:** Riojas, Abel. "Jodie Foster, Reluctant Star."

60 Minutes, December 7, 1999, accessed June 6, 2016, http://www.cbsnews.com/news/jodie-foster-reluctant-star-07-12-1999.

40 **Matt Damon:** "The Inner Actor: The Personal Side of Performing," accessed June 6, 2016, http://theinneractor.com/111/feeling-like-a-fraud.

40 **Sheryl Sandberg:** Miller, Linda Hagen. "The Confidence Ceiling: Why Do So Many Women Have Such a Hard Time Believing in Themselves?" *Inlander*, February 6, 2015, accessed June 6, 2016, http://www.inlander.com/spokane/the-confidence-ceiling/Content?oid=2407688.

40 **Alan Dye:** Edwards, Jim. "One of Apple's Top Designers Gave a Marvelous Quote About How Stressful It Is to Work at Apple." *Business Insider*, September 11, 2005, accessed June 6, 2016, http://www.businessinsider.com/alan-dye-quote-about-stress-at-apple-and-imposter-syndrome-2015-9?r=UK&IR=T.

40 **a recent survey taken by Roger Jones:** Jones, Roger. "What CEOs Are Afraid Of." *Harvard Business Review*, February 24, 2015, accessed June 6, 2016, https://hbr.org/2015/02/what-ceos-are-afraid-of.

41 **Moses, the great prophet of the Bible:** Exodus 4:10.

41 **"Why do I have to do all this silly, friendly behavior?":** Quotation from my own research data.

44 **"It's a very uncomfortable feeling":** Ibid.

48 **And each time she did it:** In the end, Jessie ended up leaving the profession because of how much these types of situations grated on her—or, in her words, how "incredibly gross" she felt. Rather than develop a sense of conviction about why she was doing it, Jessie struggled to find that underlying worthy purpose—and eventually left her job.

49 **Actor Hugh Grant:** Stossel, "Performance Anxiety in Great Performers: What Hugh Grant, Gandhi, and Thomas Jefferson have in common."

49 **Another example of paralysis comes from Mahatma Gandhi:** Ibid.

52 **"my cheeks flush and I start to cry":** Brodesser-Akner, Taffy. "How to Stop Crying: Confessions of a Chronic Crier." *Huffington Post,* March 13, 2013, accessed June 5, 2016, http://www.huffingtonpost.com/2013/03/13/how-to-stop-crying-control-emotions_n_2829457.html.

Chapter 2. Our Amazing Capacity to Avoid

56 **Warren Buffett once lamented:** http://www.businessinsider.com/how-warren-buffett-learned-public-speaking-2014-12.

56 **The famous classical composer Frédéric Chopin:** "7 Famous Classical Musicians Who Suffered from Stage Fright." *CMuse*, February 15, 2015, accessed June 6, 2016, http://www.cmuse.org/famous-classical-musicians-who-suffered-from-stage-fright.

57 **In a recent survey commissioned by Age UK:** "British Workers Going to Extreme Measures to Avoid Small Talk." HR Grapevine, May 15, 2015, accessed June 6, 2015, http://www.hrgrapevine.com/markets/hr/article/2015-05-15-british-workers-going-to-extreme-measures-to-avoid-small-talk.

58 **"made him feel like Albert Brooks's sweaty, hyperventilating character in *Broadcast News*":** Stein, Alexander. "What Entrepreneurs Are Feeling: Fear." *Fortune Small Business*, December 2, 2008, accessed June 6, 2016, http://boswellgroup.com/what-entrepreneurs-are-feeling-fear.

60 **research by Larry Stybel and his colleagues on executive dismissals:** Stybel, Laurence, et al. "Planning Executive Dis-

missals: How to Fire a Friend." *California Management Review* 24 (1982): 73–80.

61 **a recent survey:** Tierney, John. "This Was Supposed to Be My Column for New Year's Day." *New York Times*, January 14, 2013, accessed July 11, 2016, http://www.nytimes.com/2013/01/15/science/positive-procrastination-not-an-oxymoron.html?_r=0.

61 **Clinton would wait weeks:** "Procrastination in Science," accessed June 6, 2016, https://procrastinus.com/procrastination/famous-procrastinators.

62 **Herman Melville:** Ibid.

64 **"You will pay for your senseless behavior":** Tahmincioglu, Eve. "Employers Maintaining Vigilance in the Face of Layoff Rage." *New York Times*, August 1, 2001, accessed June 6, 2016, http://www.nytimes.com/2001/08/01/business/01SABO.html?pagewanted=all.

64 **development process itself:** "CEOs Passing the Buck of Talent Management." accessed June 6, 2016, http://www.management-issues.com/news/4860/ceos-passing-the-buck-on-talent-management.

Chapter 3. Conviction: The Critical Importance of Having a Deep Sense of Purpose

77 **"But [people] will work hardest of all when they are dedicated to a cause":** "More from and About Harry Emerson Fosdick," accessed June 6, 2016, http://www.livinglifefully.com/people/harryemersonfosdick.htm.

79 **"I have a right to be here":** "From $1,000 to $2 Billion: How One Person Grew into a Shark." CUToday, accessed June 6, 2016, http://www.cutoday.info/THE-boost/From-1-000-To-2-Billion-How-One-Person-Grew-Into-A-Shark.

79 **dramatically changed their experience of the task:** Grant, Adam, et al. "Impact and the Art of Motivation Maintenance: The Effects of Contact with Beneficiaries on Persistence Behavior." *Organizational Behavior and Human Decision Processes* 103 (2007): 53–67.

80 **advocating for a friend or mentee:** Amanatullah, Emily, and Michael W. Morris. "Negotiating Gender Roles: Gender Differences in Assertive Negotiating Are Mediated by Women's Fear of Backlash and Attenuated When Negotiating on Behalf of Others." *Journal of Personality and Social Psychology* 98 (2010): 256–267.

85 **"for the three days leading up to the speech, I could hardly breathe":** Grant, Adam. "How I Overcame the Fear of Public Speaking." *LinkedIn Pulse*, accessed June 6, 2016, https://www.linkedin.com/pulse/20140918134337-69244073-over coming-the-fear-of-public-speaking?trk=pulse-det-nav_art.

Chapter 4. Customization: Finding Your Own Personal Way of Performing the Task

105 **more effective in situations such as job interviews:** Carney, Dana, et al. "Brief Nonverbal Displays Affect Neuroendocrine Levels and Risk Tolerance." *Psychological Science* 21 (2010): 1363–1368.

110 **"refusing any meetings before 8 a.m. or after 9 p.m.":** Clark, Dorie. "Networking for Introverts." *Harvard Business Review*, August 15, 2014, accessed June 6, 2016, https://hbr.org/2014/08/networking-for-introverts.

113 **"subdue the residual physiological eruptions that the drugs are inadequate to contain":** Stossel, Scott. "Surviving Anxiety." *Atlantic.*

117 **"Help me! Dave, help me! Help me!":** Lewis, Hilary. "Four of

Larry David's Funniest Rants From His 'Fish in the Dark' Interviews." *Hollywood Reporter*, accessed June 6, 2016, http://www.hollywoodreporter.com/news/larry-david-fish-dark-interview-779600.

117 **"How do they do this? This is crazy!":** NPR staff. "Much to His Chagrin, On Broadway Larry David Has to 'Wait and Talk.'" NPR, accessed June 6, 2016, http://whro.org/arts-entertainment/11-arts-entertainment/13769-much-to-his-chagrin-on-broadway-larry-david-has-to-wait-and-talk.

118 **"you have to abide by the script":** Interview with Terry Gross, *Fresh Air*, accessed June 6, 2016, http://www.npr.org/2015/08/27/435189228/larry-davids-first-time-on-broadway-its-not-so-easy.

118 **"'Well, I'm wearing my own clothes'":** NPR staff, "Much to His Chagrin, On Broadway Larry David Has to 'Wait and Talk.'"

121 **compared to those who weren't told their ball was lucky:** Damisch, Lysann, et al. "Keep Your Fingers Crossed! How Superstition Improves Performance." *Psychological Science* 21 (2010): 1014–1020.

122 **"I wish he'd talk about XYZ":** Branson, Richard. "Why You Need to Face Your Fears Head-On." *Daily Monitor*, accessed June 6, 2016, http://www.monitor.co.ug/Business/Prosper/-/688616/1396678/-/bqf7nb/-/index.html.

122 **Mark Twain:** Nordquist, Richard. "How Mark Twain Conquered Stage Fright." *About Education*, accessed June 6, 2016, http://grammar.about.com/od/classicessays/a/How-Mark-Twain-Conquered-Stage-Fright.htm.

123 **important protocols for staging the context:** Baile, Walter, et al. "SPIKES—A Six-Step Protocol for Delivering Bad News: Application to the Patient with Cancer." *Oncologist* 21 (2000): 302–311.

Chapter 5. Clarity: The Power
of Honest Perspective

130 **"if you've cheated the man in the glass"**: Wimbrow, Dale. "The Guy in the Glass," accessed June 6, 2016, http://www .theguyintheglass.com/gig.htm.

132 **"It's all been a big sham"**: IMDb, Michelle Pfeiffer quotes, accessed June 6, 2016, http://m.imdb.com/name/nm0000201/ quotes.

132 **"I've run a game on everybody, and they're going to find me out"**: Richards, Carl. "Learning to Deal with the Impostor Syndrome." *New York Times*, October, 26, 2015, accessed June 6, 2016, http://www.nytimes.com/2015/10/26/your-money/ learning-to-deal-with-the-impostor-syndrome.html.

134 **in his book** *Daily Rituals*: Currey, Mason. *Daily Rituals: How Artists Work* New York: Knopf, 2013.

134 **Microsoft chairman Bill Gates**: Guth, Robert A. "In Secret Hideaway, Bill Gates Ponders Microsoft's Future." *Wall Street Journal*, March 28, 2015, accessed June 6, 2016, http://www. wsj.com/article_email/SB111196625830690477-IZjgYN klaB4o52sbHmIa62Im4.htm.

136 **psychological detachment of referring to ourselves in the third person**: Weintraub, Pamela. "The Voice of Reason." *Psychology Today*, May 4, 2015, accessed June 6, 2016, https:// www.psychologytoday.com/articles/201505/the-voice-reason.

138 **Fascinating research from James Pennebaker**: Murray, Bridgett. "Writing to Heal." *APA Monitor* 33 (2002): 54.

139 **"Rejections and Failures"**: Voytek, Bradley, PhD, accessed June 6, 2016, http://bit.ly/25Iap48.

Chapter 6. The Surprising Benefits
of Taking a Leap

150 **Ella Cheng:** Lopez, Kathryn. "USG President Ella Cheng '16 Finds Success Outside the Comfort Zone." Woodrow Wilson School, June 25, 2015, accessed June 6, 2016, http://wws.princeton.edu/news-and-events/news/item/usg-president-ella-cheng-%E2%80%9916-finds-success-outside-comfort-zone.

164 *Huffington Post* **columnist Anniki Sommerville:** Sommerville, Anniki. "Five Things I've Enjoyed About Motherhood That I Never Thought I Would." *Huffington Post*, February 27, 2015, accessed June 6, 2016, http://www.huffingtonpost.co.uk/anniki-sommerville/joys-of-parenting_b_6387518.html.

165 *Lean In* **author Sheryl Sandberg:** "Transcript and Video of Speech by Sheryl Sandberg, Chief Operating Officer, Facebook, May 18, 2011," accessed June 6, 2016, http://barnard.edu/headlines/transcript-and-video-speech-sheryl-sandberg-chief-operating-officer-facebook.

171 **psychological research by Albert Bandura:** Carey, Michael P., and Andrew D. Forsyth. "Teaching Tip Sheet: Self-Efficacy, American Psychological Association," accessed June 6, 2016, http://www.apa.org/pi/aids/resources/education/self-efficacy.aspx.

Chapter 7. Building Resilience

181 **Psychologists have found:** Salas, E., and J. A. Cannon-Bowers. "The Science of Training: A Decade of progress." *Annual Review of Psychlogy* 52 (2001): 471–499.

185 **psychologist Carol Dweck:** Dweck, Carol. "Motivational Processes Affecting Learning." *American Psychologist* 41 (1986): 1040–1048.

187 **lengthy role-plays in "Hogan's Alley":** Hogan's Alley (FBI), accessed June 6, 2016, https://en.wikipedia.org/wiki/Hogan's_Alley_%28FBI%29.

188 **Adam Grant followed these principles to a T:** Grant, Adam. "How I Overcame the Fear of Public Speaking." *LinkedIn Pulse,* accessed June 6, 2016, https://www.linkedin.com/pulse/20140918134337-69244073-overcoming-the-fear-of-public-speaking?trk=pulse-det-nav_art.

190 **Richard Branson's bold advice:** Branson, Richard. "My Top 10 Quotes on Opportunity," accessed June 6, 2016, https://www.virgin.com/richard-branson/my-top-10-quotes-on-opportunity.

191 **"Drive Carefully":** Freedman, Jonathan, and Scott Fraser. "Compliance Without Pressure: The Foot-in-the-Door Technique." *Journal of Personality and Social Psychology* 4 (1966): 195–202.

194 **In her outstanding book *Mindset*:** Dweck, Carol. *Mindset: The New Psychology of Success.* New York: Random House, 2006.

197 **Teresa Amabile:** Amabile, Teresa, and Steven Kramer. *The Progress Principle: Using Small Wins to Ignite Joy, Engagement, and Creativity at Work.* Boston: Harvard Business Review Press, 2011.

211 **General Motors CEO Mary Barra's mentor:** Entis, Laura. "5 Famous Business Leaders on the Power of Mentorship." *Entrepreneur,* August 6, 2015, accessed June 6, 2016, https://www.entrepreneur.com/slideshow/249233.

211 **Steve Jobs's early career mentor Robert Friedland:** Bergelson, Mike. "Steve Jobs: A Man of Many Mentors." *Modern Workforce,* May 7, 2014, accessed June 6, 2016, https://www.geteverwise.com/mentoring/steve-jobs-a-man-of-many-mentors.

212 **Richard Branson's mentor, Freddie Laker:** Cohn, Fred. "How Celebrities Face Their Worst Fears." *Life Reimagined*, August 23, 2013, accessed June 6, 2016, http://lifereimagined .aarp.org/stories/3641-How-Celebrities-Face-Their-Worst -Fears&icid=SG-AA.

Chapter 8. The Myths and Realities

219 **psychologist Mihaly Csikszentmihalyi:** Csikszentmihalyi, Mihaly. *Flow: the Psychology of Optimal Experience.* New York: HarperPerennial Modern Classics, 2008.

219 **Edward Fenster, cofounder and chairman of Sunrun:** Ekiel Brown, Erika. "Edward Fenster: Operate Out of Your Comfort Zone." *Insights by Stanford Business*, October 14, 2015, accessed June 6, 2016, http://www.gsb.stanford.edu/insights/ edward-fenster-operate-out-your-comfort-zone.

221 **scholar Joseph Campbell:** Campbell, Joseph. *The Power of Myth.* New York: Anchor, 1991.

ACKNOWLEDGMENTS

I often joke that it's ironic that I'm writing a book about step-ping outside your comfort zone, because if you know me well, you'd know that I'm probably the last person who should be writing such a book. I'm terrible at stretching out-side my comfort zone! But perhaps because I struggle at it, I'm attuned to the challenges and can empathize with the experiences of others.

I am so grateful for the many friends and colleagues who have helped shape the ideas in this book, inspiring me to step outside my own comfort zone, and ultimately making the publication of this book possible. First, I'd like to thank my agent, Jim Levine, who has so expertly guided me through all aspects of the book publication process. Jim is smart, attentive, trustworthy—and a clear, no-nonsense type of person, who believed in me and has been such a great advocate—and source of support—throughout the entire book writing process. Ken Gillett and his entire team at Target Digital Marketing have been so fun to work with, and have been such an indispensible resource for helping me spread the word about *Reach*. My editor at Penguin/Avery, Caroline Sutton, has been an absolute pleasure to work with. Caroline has such a great sense of the flow, structure, and voice of a book . . . and I've learned so much from working with her. Brianna Flaherty has given timely and insightful feedback as well, keeping the project moving and providing expert advice along the way. Finally, I've also really enjoyed working with Avery's crackerjack team of marketers and publicists, including Lindsay Gordon, Farin Schlussel, and Louisa Farrar—and Rob Nissen as well.

I am tremendously grateful to the many professionals I spoke with when doing research for this book. They were thoughtful, candid, and extremely generous with their time and insights, and this book truly could have never happened without them. I want to also thank my students—especially those from my global dexterity classes, who stepped outside their comfort zones and courageously shared their experiences. The "R & D" for *Reach* comes from my academic colleagues, who, throughout the years, have provided invaluable support, feedback, and encouragement. All the work about necessary evils profiled here was in full collaboration with Joshua Margolis from Harvard Business School—a true friend, colleague, and scholar. Sally Maitlis has been a great friend and colleague, offering expert wisdom and a great sense of humor and perspective about life and academics. Adam Grant has helped me in innumerable ways throughout the years, offering feedback on my ideas, facilitating numerous connections with colleagues in the field, and serving as an inspiration to me as someone who so seamlessly bridges the academic-practice divide. I would also like to thank my many colleagues at Brandeis, Harvard, and beyond, who have offered such great support and friendship as I have embarked on this second book-writing adventure.

Though my academic colleagues are typically stunned when I tell them this, I actually really like writing books! And, in fact, what I like the most about it is the actual physical experience of nestling into a chair or sofa and typing on the keys. So, though I know it's a bit unorthodox, I feel compelled to acknowledge the old weathered armchair upstairs in the corner of my favorite café; the black leather sofa on the secret second floor of my town library; and the kitchen table, sofa, and chair in my own house. Here's where I had those wonderful experiences of losing myself in my thoughts and ideas—which, to me, is the absolute, number-one most pleasurable aspect of writing anything.

Finally, to my family: There's really no way any of this would have been possible without the love and support of my parents, my brother and sister-in-law, my in-laws, and then, of course, my own wife and kids. I am not the type to spend long nights writing or to displace other family activities with my book . . . so that wasn't really the issue in my case. It was more the constant, steady, encouraging support from my family—and especially from my wife—that mattered so much in giving me the inspiration and motivation to pour everything I had into it.

Whenever you write a book, it's a family affair. And that was definitely the case for me. My wife, Jen, was my close personal companion throughout the entire process—the person I shared all of this with—the excitement, the frustration, the uncertainty and . . . hopefully, the success! And I couldn't imagine it any other way. I also have to mention my son, Ben, who was always willing to wrestle, play basketball, or watch the Red Sox to help me blow off steam, and my daughter, Alice, who was my design and social media guru, begging me to get modern with my own YouTube channel and helping me learn Snapchat—which wasn't useful at all for this book, but which is super fun to do. And then finally our dog, Josie, who, regrettably, can't read, but does enjoy eating books—and also loves to snuggle and take walks, both of which proved to be instrumental to the book-writing process.

To everyone—and everything—that made this book possible, I am forever grateful!

Index

Illustrations are indicated by *italicized* numbers

Acting metaphor, 95–96
Addiction counselors, 81–82
Advancement, 4. *See also* Career
    advancement
Age UK, 57
Amabile, Teresa, 197
Amanatullah, Emily, 79–80
Angelou, Maya, 131–32
Anxiety, 38
Assertiveness
    behavior sticking for, 184
    by Jones, 185–86, 199
    practice of, 184
Attempting stage
    slipup in, 202–3
    taking a leap for, 201–2
Authenticity challenge
    of Kennedy, 12–13
    of Leak, 169–70
    as psychological challenge, 23
    of Reddy, 25
    self-assessment for, 233
    of Singh, 27–28
Avoidance
    by buck passing, 240–41

by Buffett, 56
by Chopin, 56
clarity for, 129
consequence of, 21
emotions and, 52–53
of entire task, 236–37
evolutionary advantage of,
    55–56
by Gold, 59
as milestone, 200–201
partway task for, 58–59, 238–39
by procrastination, 239–40
by Rogers, 128–29
situational sample of, 236
of snake, 65–66
by Stein, 57–58
strategies of, 235
stress from, 66–67
vicious cycle of, *66*, 66–67
Axiom (e-commerce start-up),
    27–28

Bad news, 63
Bandura, Albert, 170–71
Barra, Mary, 211–12

Beethoven, 134
Behavior, 92–93, 245
Behavior flexing
    behavior sticking for, 180
    Branson on, 121–22
    of cultures, 10–11
    overcoming of, 17, 72, 143,
        225–26
    props for, 121–22
    staging for, 125
    struggling with, 7–8
Behavior sticking
    for assertiveness, 184
    for behavior flexing, 180
    forcing mechanisms for, 189–90
    for Jones, 183–84
    observation for, 197–98
    practice for, 181, 225–26
    resilience for, 175
"Best case" thinking
    clarity for, 251–52
    situation and, 253–54
Body language
    customization by, 104, 247–48
    of Jones, 104–5
    of Lodge, 106–7
Book review, 142–43
Brain scans, 137
Branson, Richard
    advice by, 190–91
    on behavior flexing, 121–22
    Laker mentoring of, 211–12
Breaking point, 32
Britten, Benjamin, 134
Brockner, Joel, 209–10
Buck passing
    avoidance by, 240–41
    for bad news, 63
    by organization leaders, 64
    Paese on, 64
    sabotage from, 63–64
Buffett, Warren, 56
Business school, 35–36

Campbell, Joseph, 221
Capable person, 218
Career advancement, 243
Carney, Dana, 105–6
Celebrities, 37–38, 40
Challenges. See also Authenticity
        challenge; Competence
        challenge; Incremental
        challenges; Likeability
        challenge; Morality
        challenge; Portfolio
        challenges; Psychological
        challenge; Resentment
        challenge
    of comfort zone, 12, 48, 71–72,
        213
    emotions influenced by, 49
    goal influenced by, 1–2
    guideline for, 7–8
    of Jones, 3, 182–83
    normalization of, 222–23
    of public speaking, 8
    small steps for, 192–93
    of Thao, 161
Chang, Lily
    competence challenge of, 13
    conviction of, 84–85
    morality challenge of, 14, 44–45
    nervousness of, 1
    stepping away by, 134–35
    timing by, 111
Cheng, Ella
    for class president, 150–52
    against self-promotion, 150–51
    support system of, 209
Chopin, Frédéric, 56
Clarity
    attainment of, 133
    for avoidance, 129
    for "best case" thinking, 251–52
    coach for, 140–41
    for distorted thinking, 130–32
    by Hackman, 141–42

positive cycle of, *153*, 153–54
by realistic thinking, 252–53
as resource, 15–16, 73–74
stepping away for, 133–34
third-person pronoun for, 136
for "worst case" thinking,
    251–52
Clark, Dorie, 108–10
Class participation, 7–8
Class president, 150–52
Classroom debates, 159–60
Clinton, Bill, 61–62
Coach
    for clarity, 140–41
    for Evans, 140–41, 208–9
    Hackman as, 141–42, 209–10
    practice with, 184–85
Cohen, Jennifer, 113–15
Collaboration, 43, 199
Comfort zone
    challenges of, 12, 48, 71–72, 213
    confronting of, 1–2
    cross-cultural code-switching
        and, 10–11
    of David, 117–18
    diagram of, *4*, 5–6, 143, 216–17
    discovery influence on, 162–63
    distorted thinking of, 131
    of Fenster, 219–20
    "Get Out of Your Comfort
        Zone: A Guide for the
        Terrified" on, 11–12
    Global Dexterity on, 10–11
    for goal achievement, 5
    on Google, 4–5
    hype of, 213
    in ideal world, 3
    of Kennedy, 2
    life analogy for, 226–27
    of Linden, 179–80
    myth of, 214
    portfolio of, 205–6
    of professions, 16–17

psychological challenges of, 21,
    23
small commitments for, 191–92
small steps for, 192
taking a leap for, 72–73
universal phenomenon of,
    220–21
Company culture, 28–29
Competence challenge
    of business school, 35–36
    of celebrities, 37–38, 40
    of Chang, 13
    impostor syndrome of, 38–39
    Lodge of, 36–37
    as psychological challenge, 24
    self-assessment for, 233
Complementary skills, 219
Considering stage, 200–201
Context, customization by, 250–51
Conviction
    of addiction counselors, 81–82
    Amanatullah on, 79–80
    by career advancement, 243
    of Chang, 84–85
    of Corcoran, 78–79
    flexible framework for, 143–44
    Fosdick on, 77
    of Grant, A., 85–86
    of Harris, 87
    by helping others, 244
    of Jones, 82–84
    of Leak, 168–69
    Morris on, 79–80
    necessary evils influenced by,
        80–81
    of pediatric physicians, 82
    of police officers, 80–81
    positive cycle of, *153*, 153–54
    as resource, 14–15, 73–74
    by respect, 243
    by self-esteem boosting, 244
    by skill development, 243
    sources of, 78–79, 242

Conviction (*cont.*)
  of taking a leap, 160–61
  by Warren, 76–78
  of Wong, J., 257*n*48
Corcoran, Barbara, 78–79
Courage, 180
Cross-cultural code-switching,
    10–11
Crying, 51–52
Csikszentmihalyi, Mihaly, 219
Cuddy, Amy, 105–6
Cultures, 10–11. *See also* Company
    culture
Currey, Mason, 134
Customization
  acting metaphor for, 95–96
  of behavior, 92–93, 245
  by body language, 104, 247–48
  by Cohen, 113–15
  by context, 250–51
  by Dater, 102
  by dialogue, 245–46
  empowerment from, 96–97
  flexible framework of, 143–44
  by Gupta, 98–100
  of language, 93, 97
  by Leak, 169
  by location, 124
  by Maker, 103–4, 122–23
  positive cycle of, *153*, 153–54
  by props, 113–14, 249–50
  by Reddy, 98
  of refining stage, 202–4
  as resource, 15, 73–74
  of seating arrangement, 94
  tailor metaphor for, 95
  of timing, 107–8, 248–49
  by Wong, L., 91–92

Daily Rituals (Currey), 134
Dater, Brenda
  customization by, 102
  expert role by, 100–102

Parenting Without Panic by,
    100–101
  personal stories by, 102–3
David, Larry
  comfort zone of, 117–18
  costume of, 118–19
  scripted play by, 117–18
Diagram, of comfort zone, *4*, 5–6,
    143, 216–17
Dialogue, 245–46
Discovery
  comfort zone influenced by,
    162–63
  of doing better, 165–66
  by Evans, 170
  of fatherhood, 165–67
  by Jones, 170
  necessary evils and, 161–62
  by Nickerson, 170
  trying by, 149–50
Distorted thinking
  by Angelou, 131–32
  clarity for, 130–32
  of comfort zone, 131
  by Pfeiffer, 131–32
Doing better, 165–66
Dress style, 29
"Drive Carefully" study, 191
Dweck, Carol
  "learning orientation" by,
    184–85
  Mindset by, 194

Easy Family Travel, 127–28
Emotional overload, 51–52
Emotions
  avoidance and, 52–53
  challenges influence on, 49
  job incompetence from, 50
  necessary evils influence on, 51
Empowerment, 96–97
Enjoying stage, 204–5
Entrepreneur, 177–78

Evans, Roger
    coach for, 140–41, 208–9
    collaboration by, 43, 199
    discovery by, 170
    props by, 115–16
    resentment challenge of, 42–43
    support system of, 208–9
    transformation by, 163–64
Exaggerated thinking. *See*
        Distorted thinking
Existential angst, 86–87
Expert role, 100–102

Father, 209–11
Fatherhood, 165–67
Fear
    of fatherhood, 165–67
    of trying, 149
Fenster, Edward, 219–20
Firing
    of Julia, 1–2, 44–45, 134–35
    professional pride of, 162
Fixed mind-set
    growth mind-set and, 196
    learning process influenced by,
        194
Flexible framework
    for conviction, 143–44
    of customization, 143–44
    of self-reflection, 143–44
"Flow," 219
Forcing mechanisms, 189–90
Fosdick, Harry Emerson, 77
Fraser, Scott, 191
Freedman, Jonathan, 191
Friedland, Robert, 211–12
Fund-raising, 79

Gandhi, Mahatma, 49
Gates, Bill, 134
"Get Out of Your Comfort Zone: A
        Guide for the Terrified"
        (Molinsky), 11–12

Give and Take (Grant, A.), 188–89
Global Dexterity (Molinsky), 10–11
Goal
    challenge influence on, 1–2
    comfort zone for, 5
Goat's milk soap
    by Linden, 177–78
    manager against, 179
Gold, Dan
    avoidance by, 59
    capable person for, 218
    partway task by, 59–60
Google, 4–5
Gosling, Alan, 45
Grant, Adam
    conviction of, 85–86
    for fund-raising, 79
    Give and Take by, 188–89
    on public speaking, 85
    on setting realism, 188–89
Grant, Hugh, 49
Growth mind-set
    fixed mind-set and, 196
    learning process influenced by,
        194
    of Rose, 195–96
Guideline, 7–8
Gupta, Sangita, 98–100
"The Guy in the Glass"
        (Wimbrow), 129–30

Hackman, Richard
    book review by, 142–43
    clarity by, 141–42
    as coach, 141–42, 209–10
Harris, Barbara
    conviction of, 87
    existential angst by, 86–87
    last rites by, 86
Helping others, 244
"Hero's journey"
    by Campbell, 221
    crafting of, 221–22

Hewlett, William, 219
"Hogan's Alley," 187–88
Home, situation at, 232
Housebreaking, 193–94
Huffington Post, 51–52
Hype, 213

Impostor syndrome
  of competence challenge,
    38–39
  of Moses, 40–41
  of Portman, 39
  by Warren, 75–76
Income, 147–48
Incremental challenges, 181–82
Inspiration, 225
Interrogation, 25–26

Jenna (author colleague), 124–25
Jesus (savior lookalike), 157–58
Jobs, Steve
  Friedland mentoring of, 211–12
  Wozniak and, 219
Jones, Annie
  assertiveness by, 185–86, 199
  behavior sticking for, 183–84
  body language of, 104–5
  breaking point of, 32
  challenges of, 3, 182–83
  conviction of, 82–84
  discovery by, 170
  likeability challenge of, 13, 31
  resentment challenge of, 13, 42
  transformation of, 162–63
Julia (best friend), 1–2, 44–45,
  134–35
"Just right" challenge
  commitment to, 190–91
  practice of, 182

Kennedy, Neil
  authenticity challenge of, 12–13
  comfort zone of, 2

procrastination by, 62
  website by, 2
Kramer, Steven, 197
Kross, Ethan, 136–37

Laker, Freddie, 211–12
Language, 93, 97
Last rites, 86
Leak, Phil
  authenticity challenge of, 169–70
  conviction of, 168–69
  customization by, 169
  taking a leap by, 167–68
"Learning orientation," 184–85
Learning process, 194
Likeability challenge
  of Jones, 13, 31
  of Maxwell, 33–34
  positive feedback of, 30–31
  as psychological challenge, 24
  self-assessment for, 234
  of social media, 34–35
Linden, Sara
  comfort zone of, 179–80
  competition scoping by, 178
  courage of, 180
  as entrepreneur, 177–78
  goat's milk soap by, 177–78
  support system of, 207–8
Location
  customization by, 124
  Jenna use of, 124–25
Lodge, Wendy
  body language of, 106–7
  of competence challenge, 36–37
  timing by, 107–8
Lucky charm, 119–21
Lyons, Drew
  resentment challenge of, 41–42
  timing by, 110–11

"Magic" outside, 216
Mahler, Gustav, 134

Maker, Leslie
  customization by, 103–4, 122–23
  timing by, 111–12
Margolis, Joshua, 255*n*9
Maxwell, Dan, 33–34
Medical school student
  morality challenge of, 45–46
  on necessary evils, 46–47
Medicine, staging in, 122–23
Melville, Herman, 61–62
Milestone
  avoiding stage as, 200–201
  considering stage as, 200–201
  for progress measurement, 200,
    205
Mindset (Dweck), 194
Molinsky, Andy
  "Get Out of Your Comfort
    Zone: A Guide for the
    Terrified," 11–12
  Global Dexterity by, 10–11
Morality challenge
  of Chang, 14, 44–45
  of Gosling, 45
  of medical school student,
    45–46
  as psychological challenge, 24
  self-assessment for, 234
  of Wong, J., 47–48, 257*n*48
Morris, Michael W., 79–80
Moses (Bible prophet), 40–41
Motherhood, 164–65
Myth
  of comfort zone, 214
  of inspiration, 225
  of "magic" outside, 216
  of only one, 220
  of "sucking it up," 223
  of taking a leap, 214–16

Necessary evils
  conviction influence on, 80–81
  discovery and, 161–62
  emotions influenced by, 51
  by Margolis, 255n9
  medical school student on, 46–47
  partway task of, 60–61
  of pediatric physicians, 198–99
  of work, 9–10
Negotiation, 79–80
Nickerson, Amanda
  career path of, 146
  discovery by, 170
  income for, 147–48
  at interview, 145
  résumé of, 146–47
  self-promotion of, 147
  taking a leap by, 148–49
The No Asshole Rule (Sutton), 31–32

Observation, 197–98
Only one, 220
Organizational change, 8–9
Organization leaders, 64

Packard, Dave, 219
Paese, Matt, 64
Paralysis, 49
Parenting Without Panic (Dater),
  100–101
Partnerships, 219
Partway task
  avoidance through, 58–59,
    238–39
  by Gold, 59–60
  of necessary evils, 60–61
  by Stybel, 60–61
Pediatric physicians
  conviction of, 82
  necessary evils of, 198–99
Pennebaker, James, 138–39
Pep talk, 111
Personal stories, 102–3
Pfeiffer, Michelle, 131–32
Pig, kissing of, 168–69
Police officers, 80–81

Portfolio challenges
    of comfort zone, 205–6
    confidence from, 206
Portman, Natalie, 39
Positive cycle
    of clarity, *153*, 153–54
    of conviction, *153*, 153–54
    of customization, *153*, 153–54
Positive feedback, 30–31
"Power pose"
    Carney on, 105–6
    Cuddy on, 105–6
    Yap on, 105–6
Practice
    of assertiveness, 184
    for behavior sticking, 181, 225–26
    with coach, 184–85
    of incremental challenges, 181–82
    of "just right" challenge, 182
    by setting realism, 186–87
Preparation, 112–13
Presentation delivery, 29–30
Procrastination
    avoidance by, 239–40
    by Clinton, 61–62
    by Melville, 61–62
Prodigy, 89–90
Professional pride, 162
Professions, 16–17
Progress measurement, 200, 205
The Progress Principle (Amabile
        and Kramer), 197
Props
    for behavior flexing, 121–22
    by Cohen, 114–15
    customization by, 113–14,
        249–50
    by Evans, 115–16
    examples of, 116–17
    lucky charm for, 119–21
    for public speaking, 119
Psychological challenge
    authenticity challenge as, 23

of comfort zone, 21, 23
    competence challenge as, 24
    likeability challenge as, 24
    morality challenge as, 24
    resentment challenge as, 24
Public speaking
    challenge of, 8
    Grant, A., on, 85
    props for, 119
    Twain on, 122

Realistic thinking
    clarity by, 252–53
    situation and, 253–54
Reddy, Jane
    authenticity challenge of, 25
    customization by, 98
    interrogation by, 25–26
    methods of, 26–27
    stepping away by, 134–35
Refining stage, 202–4
"Rejections and Failures" CV,
        139–40
Resentment challenge
    of Evans, 42–43
    of Jones, 13, 42
    of Lyons, 41–42
    as psychological challenge, 24
    self-assessment for, 233–34
Resilience, 175
Resource
    clarity as, 15–16, 73–74
    conviction as, 14–15, 73–74
    customization as, 15, 73–74
Respect, 243
Résumé, of Nickerson, 146–47
Rogers, Linda
    avoidance by, 128–29
    Easy Family Travel by, 127–28
Rose, Lisa
    failure by, 195
    growth mind-set of, 195–96
    against imperfection, 194–95

Saint Nick interaction, 158–59
Scaffolding, 73–74
Schmitz, Rick, 31, 42, 82–83, 104,
        162–63, 170
"Scribe," 94
Scripted play, 117–18
Seating arrangement, 94
Self-assessment
    for authenticity challenge, 233
    for competence challenge, 233
    for likeability challenge, 234
    for morality challenge, 234
    for resentment challenge, 233–34
Self-distancing, 137–38
Self-efficacy, 170–71
Self-esteem boosting, 244
Self-promotion
    Cheng against, 150–51
    of Nickerson, 147
Self-reflection
    flexible framework of, 143–44
    by Pennebaker, 138–39
Senior faculty, 7–8
Setting realism
    Grant, A., on, 188–89
    of "Hogan's Alley," 187–88
    practice by, 186–87
    for scary situation, 188–89
Singh, Jasmit
    authenticity challenge of, 27–28
    at Axiom, 27–28
    company culture of, 28–29
    dress style of, 29
    presentation delivery of, 29–30
Situation
    "best case" thinking and, 253–54
    at home, 232
    naming of, 232
    realistic thinking and, 253–54
    at work, 231
    "worst case" thinking and, 253
Skill development. *See also*
        Complementary skills

for advancement, 4
    conviction by, 243
Small commitments
    for comfort zone, 191–92
    rule of, 189–90
Small steps
    for challenges, 192–93
    for comfort zone, 192
    rule of, 189–90
    of taking a leap, 215
Small talk
    Age UK on, 57
    Wagner and, 156–59
Small wins, 196–97
Social media, 34–35
Sommerville, Anniki, 164–65
Speaking up, 90–91
Staging
    for behavior flexing, 125
    in medicine, 122–23
Stein, Alexander, 57–58
Stepping away
    by Britten, 134
    by Chang, 134–35
    for clarity, 133–34
    by Gates, 134
    by Mahler, 134
    by Reddy, 134–35
Stossel, Scott
    anxiety of, 38
    preparation by, 112–13
Stress, 66–67
Stybel, Larry, 60–61
Success, 217–18
"Sucking it up"
    myth of, 223
    necessity of, 223–25
    as tool, 223–24
Support system
    of Barra, 211–12
    Brockner as, 209–10
    of Cheng, 209
    of Evans, 208–9

Support system (*cont.*)
  father as, 209–11
  of Linden, 207–8
Sutton, Bob, 31–32

Tailor metaphor, 95
Taking a leap
  for attempting stage, 201–2
  for comfort zone, 72–73
  conviction of, 160–61
  epiphanies from, 155
  by Leak, 167–68
  myth of, 214–16
  new view from, 153
  by Nickerson, 148–49
  power of, *153*, 154–55
  results of, 152–53
  small steps of, 215
Teaching, 204–5
Thao (Vietnamese MBA student)
  classroom debates by, 159–60
  overcoming challenge by, 161
  transformation of, 159
Third person pronoun
  brain scans of, 137
  for clarity, 136
  Kross on, 136–37
  self-distancing by, 137–38
Timing
  by Chang, 111
  by Clark, 108–10
  customization of, 107–8, 248–49
  by Lodge, 107–8
  by Lyons, 110–11
  by Maker, 111–12
  as pep talk, 111
  of success, 217–18
Transformation
  by Evans, 163–64
  of Jones, 162–63
  of Sommerville, 164–65
  of Thao, 159

Trying
  fear of, 149
  by personal discovery, 149–50
Twain, Mark, 122

Universal phenomenon, of
    comfort zone, 220–21

Voytek, Bradley, 139–40
Vygotsky, Lev, 73–74

Wagner, Jack
  as barista, 155–56
  Jesus interaction with, 157–58
  Saint Nick interaction with,
    158–59
  small talk and, 156–59
Warren, Lisa
  conviction by, 76–78
  impostor syndrome by, 75–76
Wimbrow, Dale, 129–30
Women, 79–80
Wong, Jessie
  conviction of, 257n48
  morality challenge of, 47–48,
    257n48
Wong, Lucy
  customization by, 91–92
  as prodigy, 89–90
  quitting by, 91
  as "scribe," 94
  speaking up by, 90–91
Work
  Necessary evils of, 9–10
  situation at, 231
"Worst case" thinking
  clarity for, 251–52
  situation and, 253
Wozniak, Steve, 219

Yap, Andy, 105–6